INTERACTIVE WRITING

STUDENT'S BOOK

Other titles of interest include

ADAMS, L. and A. LLANAS
Start Reading
Go On Reading

BADDOCK, B.
Scoop
Professional Writing

HAINES, S.
English in Print

KNIGHT, M.
Keep in Touch

MUMFORD, S.
Conversation Pieces
In the Mood

MURRAY, H. and A.M.J. NIETHAMMER-STOTT
Murder Comes to Breakfast
The Chorley Kidnapping

ZINKIN, T.
Write Right

INTERACTIVE WRITING

AN ADVANCED COURSE IN WRITING SKILLS

STUDENT'S BOOK

Editor
ANNA KWAN-TERRY

Co-editors
CATHERINE COOK   PETER H. RAGAN

in association with
The English Language Proficiency Unit,
National University of Singapore

Advisory Editor
JOHN SINCLAIR

> ENGLISH LANGUAGE UNIT
> APPLIED LANGUAGES CENTRE
> UNIVERSITY OF BATH,
> CLAVERTON DOWN,
> BATH, BA2 7AY,
> GREAT BRITAIN.

Prentice Hall

ENGLISH LANGUAGE TEACHING

New York London Toronto Sydney Tokyo Singapore

First published 1988 by
Prentice Hall International (UK) Ltd
Campus 400, Maylands Avenue
Hemel Hempstead
Hertfordshire HP2 7EZ
A division of
Simon & Schuster International Group

© 1988 Prentice Hall International (UK) Ltd

All rights reserved. No part of this publication may be reproduced, stored in a retrieval system, or transmitted, in any form, or by any means, electronic, mechanical, photocopying, recording or otherwise, without the prior permission, in writing, from the publisher.
For permission within the United States of America contact Prentice Hall Inc., Englewood Cliffs, NJ 07632.

Printed and bound in Great Britain at the
University Press, Cambridge

Library of Congress Cataloging-in-Publication Data

Kwan-Terry, Anna, 1942–
 Interactive writing.
 1. English language–rhetoric.   2. English language–
Textbooks for foreign speakers.   I. Cook, Catherine,
1949–   II. Ragan, Peter, 1944–   III. Title
 PE1408.K86   1988   808'.042   87-32793
  ISBN 0-13-469263-2
  ISBN 0-13-469305-1 (teacher's book)

British Library Cataloguing in Publication Data

Kwan-Terry, Anna
 Interactive writing: an advanced course in writing skills.
 1. English language – Textbooks for foreign speakers
  2. English language – Writing
 I. Title   II. Cook, Catherine   III. Ragan, Peter H.   IV.
 National University of Singapore. *English Language
 Proficiency Unit*
  808'.042   PE1128

 ISBN 0-13-469263-2

---

4 5 6 7 8   97 96 95 94 93

The Editor and Co-editors would like to express their gratitude to their colleagues in the Materials Writing Project of the English Language Proficiency Unit of the National University of Singapore, for their work in drafting and revising the materials which are now published for the international market.

CONTRIBUTORS

Michael Brown   Siew Hean Read
Geoffrey Crewes   Susheela Varghese
Judith Lindley   William Wong
Graham Lock

ACKNOWLEDGEMENTS

Every effort has been made to contact copyright holders and our thanks are extended to the following for permission to reproduce copyright material: Reuters, Hodder & Stoughton, Walter Damtoft, Souvenir Press, and Newsweek Inc.

CONTENTS

Preface ix
Introduction xi
To the teacher xiii

UNIT ONE
Interaction in the text: the paragraph 1

TASK 1	Introducing and developing the main point	2
TASK 2	Different ways of developing the main point	4
TASK 3	Developing each paragraph within a text	6
TASK 4	Unity of ideas in a paragraph	7
TASK 5	Planning and writing an article	8
TASK 6	Free writing	10

UNIT TWO
Interaction in the text: the complete text 11

TASK 1	Unity and coherence in a text	12
TASK 2	Supporting and developing the central theme of a text using the main points of the paragraphs	14
TASK 3	Adequate conclusions	16
TASK 4	'Intermediate' conclusions	20
TASK 5	Relating a central theme, 'intermediate' conclusions and final conclusion	22
TASK 6	Report-writing: relation of introduction, supporting paragraphs and conclusion to central theme	25
TASK 7	Writing a complete text with introduction, body and final conclusion	28

UNIT THREE
Interaction with the reader: meeting the needs of the reader 29

TASK 1	A response: the selection of appropriate information from one text to be incorporated in another	30
TASK 2	The identification of information needed by the reader	31
TASK 3	The adequate development of ideas to be clearly expressed and explicitly linked	32

TASK 4	Giving directions: making adequate assumptions	34
TASK 5	Incorporating necessary background information	35
TASK 6	Considering the purpose in writing	40
TASK 7	Writing a review	42

UNIT FOUR
Interaction with the reader: presenting a point of view   43

TASK 1	Selecting and interpreting facts to present a particular point of view	44
TASK 2	Presenting information: impersonal and objective, personalised and subjective	46
TASK 3	Further objective and subjective practice	49
TASK 4	Relationship and attitude to the reader	51
TASK 5	Assessment of topic, purpose in writing and relationship with the reader	56
TASK 6	Presenting a point of view	58

UNIT FIVE
Interaction with the reader: anticipating the reader's response   59

TASK 1	Argument and counter-argument	60
TASK 2	Presenting a convincing argument anticipating the reader's response	62
TASK 3	Dealing with counter-arguments	65
TASK 4	Elaborating a personal viewpoint: anticipating and dealing with counter-arguments	66
TASK 5	Disagreeing	69
TASK 6	Arguing for or against	70

Appendix 1   Lake Nios – text with revision notation   71

Appendix 2   Alligator River   72

PREFACE

This book has arisen from a project to improve the writing of university students. A growing number of students at the National University of Singapore have a good command of the grammar of English but lack training in the skills necessary for coherent and effective writing. Hence a materials project to provide this training was initiated in the English Language Proficiency Unit and supported by the University. The project team consisted of ten members under my leadership; Professor J.M. Sinclair of the University of Birmingham acted as consultant. Begun in January 1980, the Project took more than three years to complete, progressing through needs analysis to repeated drafting, piloting, and revision of the materials. At the end of this period the materials had essentially the shape, content and character of the final production, and full credit must be given to the original project team for their creative industry and contribution.

When the prospect arose of publishing a book for an international market, it was decided that a small editing group would accomplish the task most efficiently, and the materials were extensively revised for a wider audience.

Thanks are due to the Administration of the National University of Singapore for help and support. Special acknowledgement is due to the late Vice-Chancellor, Mr Kwan Sai Keong, whose interest and enthusiasm enabled the project to be carried out.

Singapore   *Anna Kwan-Terry*
March 1988   *Editor and Project Leader*

INTRODUCTION

WHO THIS BOOK IS FOR

This book has been specifically prepared for advanced students of writing. It is assumed that you are already well versed in basic writing skills and have a good command of grammar and vocabulary. You should already be familiar with writing in a variety of ways. This book will help you to refine your ability to write coherent texts – letters, reports, reviews, articles and academic essays – which fulfil your purpose for writing and meet the needs of your reader.

WHAT THIS BOOK IS ABOUT

Two areas of interaction in writing are explored:

- In the units on 'Interaction in the Text' you will study how different parts of a paragraph interact and how paragraphs interact to form a coherent and well organised complete text.
- In the units on 'Interaction with the Reader' you will study how to take account of the reader of your text according to your purpose for writing. This involves meeting the needs of your reader for information on your topic, presenting a point of view to your reader and anticipating your reader's response to what you have written.

HOW THIS BOOK IS ORGANISED

Each unit covers different aspects of interaction in writing. In each one you will find six or seven tasks involving the reading and writing of different texts.

The first few tasks in each unit introduce you to the teaching points by presenting texts for analysis and discussion. As you proceed through each unit, the tasks provide you with increasing opportunity to contribute to the content of your writing. The final task in each unit is a writing activity which allows you freedom to use your own ideas to apply what you have learned in the unit.

Throughout each unit you will do much of the work of preparation, evaluation, and revision in groups but most of your writing individually. The interaction with other students will encourage you to share what you already know with your fellow students. The individual work, while making use of what you have learned in group discussion, will help you to become more independent in using your advanced writing skills.

In each task you are encouraged to write a rough draft and show it to other students for evaluation. You should use the comments of your readers to help you edit the draft and produce a final text which is both well organised and which caters for the needs of your reader. Almost all good writers employ this technique of drafting and editing. The comments of your fellow students will help you to become more critical of your own writing.

TO THE TEACHER

PURPOSE

The aim of *Interactive Writing* is to help advanced students of writing with writing at the discourse level. There is no formal teaching of discrete grammar points, of sentence level structures, or of the main patterns of development of ideas. It is assumed that students can already handle these and are ready to refine their writing through a detailed consideration of the relationship of ideas in a text and of the relationship between writer, purpose for writing and reader.

ORGANISATION

The book explores two areas of interaction in writing.

Interaction in the Text

- Unit One – **The Paragraph** – deals with unity and coherence in the development of main ideas at paragraph level.
- Unit Two – **The Complete Text** – continues work on the development of ideas with a study of the relationship of parts of a text to one another and to the central theme.

Interaction with the Reader

- Unit Three – **Meeting the Needs of the Reader** – is concerned with the need for a writer, when writing about a given topic for a specific purpose, to assess and make assumptions about the reader's need for information.
- Unit Four – **Presenting a Point of View** – highlights various ways in which a point of view can be communicated in a text. It covers the selective use of facts to support a given point of view, the distinction between objective and 'personalised' writing and the way a writer's attitude to his reader is revealed through tone.
- Unit Five – **Anticipating the Reader's Response** – focuses on presenting a balanced point of view which avoids exaggeration and deals with possible objections or counter-arguments.

CONTROL

The approach is largely student-centred with an emphasis on group work. The tasks at the beginning of each unit are more closely controlled than those at the end in terms of guidance given to the student and content of the text produced. The initial tasks in each unit present the teaching points. In these, students are given an example of a successfully written text (in one case contrasted with an unsuccessful one) which they analyse with the help of questions designed to highlight the teaching points. The tasks in the middle of each unit give detailed guidance to the students in both analysis and application of the teaching points. In all these earlier tasks the content is provided by the materials. By the time they reach the final task, students assume full responsibility for the content and the presentation.

(Unit Four differs in that tasks presenting teaching points alternate with those where students apply them.)

METHODOLOGY

Group Work

Another aspect of interaction which is central to the book is student interaction. While the final written text is, in most of the tasks, the responsibility of the individual student, all the preparation for writing and much of the editing is to be done as group work. This both helps to generate and enrich ideas and utilises and stimulates the growing expertise of the advanced writer. Furthermore, in line with the intention to get away from always having the teacher as addressee, the group work helps to make students aware of other audiences and to have a responsive relationship with the reader. It also frees the teacher to assume a responsive, resource-oriented role in support of the students' growing independence.

Peer Evaluation

Great emphasis is laid on peer evaluation and editing. In most of the tasks each student is expected to make some critical judgement of a text other than his own. Reading a text by another student affords a certain objectivity students may lack initially in reading their own work. This in turn makes students more critical of their own work, encourages them to be more analytical and helps them to edit their own work more efficiently. Where there are difficulties with editing, the teacher, of course, is always present to offer direction. It is at this point that areas of weakness are highlighted and the teacher can choose to supplement the materials with formal teaching of grammar and structure if this is felt to be necessary.

CONTENT

There is considerable variety within each unit. Students are presented with whole and partial texts of various types, graphics, pictures and statistics. The writing they produce includes whole or parts of letters, reports, reviews, articles and academic essays.

MANAGEMENT

Organisation of Groups

Students will quickly become used to the group work approach employed throughout the book and will probably be able to organise themselves quickly and efficiently to perform a task. Nevertheless, as always with group work, it remains the teacher's responsibility to control the groups with regard to size and ability range according to teaching aims and the abilities and personalities within a class.

Drafting and Editing

The importance of drafting and rewriting in the production of a successful text cannot be over-emphasised. Students are encouraged to go through these procedures for most of the written tasks in the book. For this reason the tasks here may take much longer to cover than is at first apparent.

Guidelines for students to use in the evaluation of each other's draft texts have been included to highlight the teaching points wherever relevant. Where such guidelines are not given, teachers are urged to guide the students through evaluation and editing of their drafts with emphasis on the teaching points of the unit. It is suggested that students should at least reach the point of discussing each other's first draft in class. However, it may not always be practical to go through the whole process of producing a text – discussion, planning, drafting, evaluation and rewriting – in class. Where it is more practical, the final draft can be done out of class as long as students are made aware of the value of peer evaluation and the fact that they should respond fully to the comments they have received in group work when producing their final draft.

Final Assessment

In most cases the final draft should be handed in to the teacher for assessment and grading.

For further feedback at the end of a writing task the teacher may find it useful to provide copies of a particularly good or a particularly weak piece of work for class discussion.

UNIT ONE

INTERACTION IN THE TEXT

THE PARAGRAPH

There must be unity of ideas in every paragraph. In other words, there is a main idea – which contributes to the central theme of the entire text – and every point in the paragraph must support and develop that idea. The main idea or point is usually some kind of general statement which is expressed explicitly in one or two sentences of the paragraph. It is developed by more specific supporting points, which may be of various kinds. The ideas can move in either direction, i.e. from general to specific or specific to general, at any point in the paragraph. Every supporting point should be adequately developed and only those that are directly relevant to the main point should be included.

TASK ONE

INTRODUCING AND DEVELOPING THE MAIN POINT

This task looks at how the main point of a paragraph is developed. The paragraphs here show some of the many ways in which specific details can support a main point.

1   The first paragraph is taken from a magazine article. As you read it, think about these questions and then discuss your answers in groups:

(a) The main point of this paragraph is expressed in a general statement. What is the main point?
(b) This main point is developed by supporting points which provide specific evidence for the generalisation. What are the supporting points?

Notice how, in this case, the more specific points follow the generalisation.

Garlic
Not to be sniffed at

Did she take the tablets?

[1]Garlic, the terror of vampires and delight of French food lovers, is making a dramatic impact on the health food industry. [2]Gone is any stigma attached to its smell; instead garlic health products are going down a treat. [3]A Japanese 'deodorised' garlic preparation, launched in America in 1982, achieved sales of $20m a year within two years. [4]Britons, who are popularly supposed to dislike garlic in food, swallow about 300 million capsules of garlic oil a year. [5]America trebled its garlic output between 1980 and 1982. [6]Even the pharmaceutical industry is taking a cautious sniff.

2   The next paragraph comes from a chapter entitled 'Pain' in a book about the human body. Again, read it and answer the questions. As you answer the questions fill in the boxes in the diagram. It will show you how the ideas interact to develop and support the main point. This is another example of a paragraph which moves from general to specific.

REACTIONS TO PAIN

However, people's reactions to pain vary. Different people have different tolerance levels. What seems intolerable to one person may not bother another, even though both feel pain. And while pain causes anguish, depression, nausea, and tears in some people, others exhibit no such effects. Even in the same person, tolerance of pain may vary with circumstances and psychological state. If you should stub your toe while running from a fierce dog or an armed robber, it probably would not hurt at all. In hospitals, medical personnel have discovered that preoperative psychological preparation seems to reduce postoperative pain: patients who are told in advance how much pain to expect and just how they are likely to feel for how long, generally need fewer painkillers after surgery than do unprepared patients.

(a) What is the main point?
(b) In developing this main point the writer classifies differences in reactions to pain into two categories. What are they?
(c) The writer gives details to support the point that reactions to pain differ from person to person. What are these details?
(d) What examples does the writer give of how a person's tolerance of pain varies?

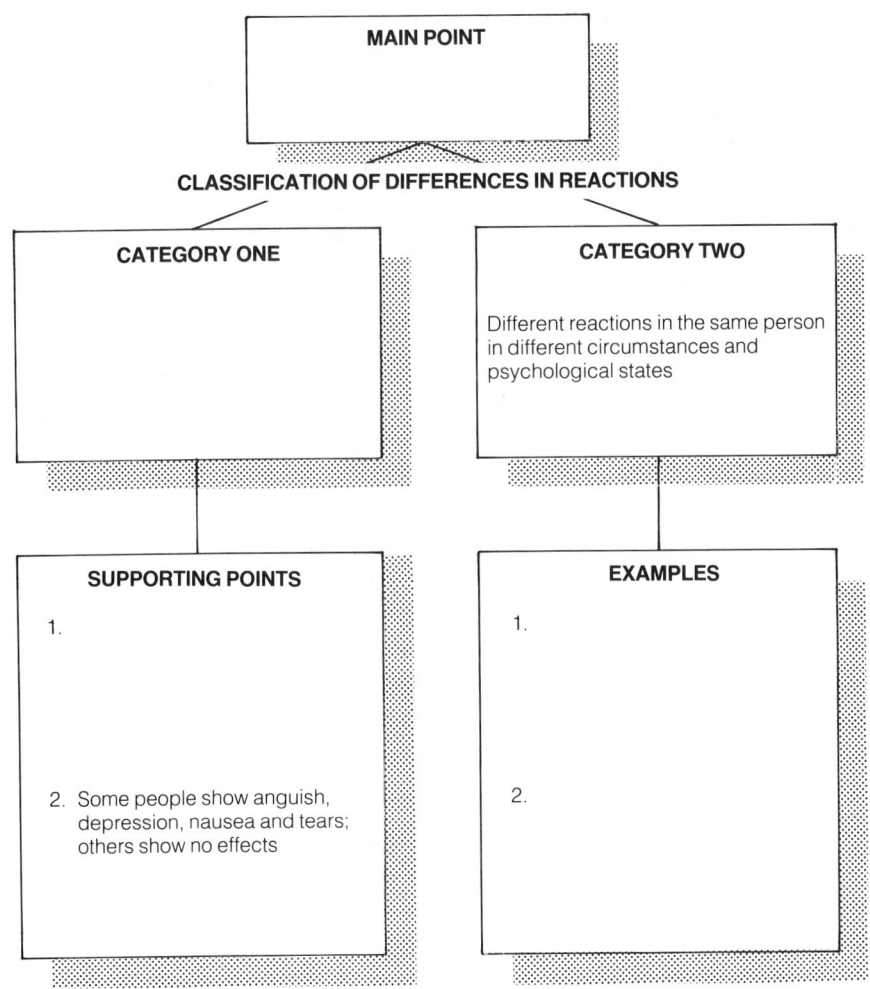

TASK TWO

DIFFERENT WAYS OF DEVELOPING THE MAIN POINT

In this task you will see some other ways of developing ideas in a paragraph and have some practice in developing and supporting a main point.

1 This paragraph comes from a chapter on volcanic eruptions in a book entitled *Natural Disasters of Our Time*. After reading it, fill in the boxes in the diagram, which shows how each sentence contributes to the development of ideas in the paragraph. Notice how the specific statements follow the main idea and then lead up to the concluding general statement.

> [1] In north-west Cameroon in August 1986, there was a volcanic eruption which caused a toxic gas leak that devastated the area. [2] At least 1,200 people were killed and many were left seriously ill with burns and respiratory infections. [3] Nobody could escape because there was no warning, just a loud explosion followed by a terrible smell like that of rotten eggs, and within a short time the entire area around Lake Nios, which was the site of the eruption, was shrouded in fumes. [4] When help came to the villages on the shores of the lake, men, women and animals were found stretched out dead: some were outside their huts, some still in bed; others were in the fields or on the village tracks. [5] It was as if a neutron bomb had exploded destroying nothing but killing all life. [6] The occurrence was the worst incident of its kind and the second time such a disaster had struck this West African nation.

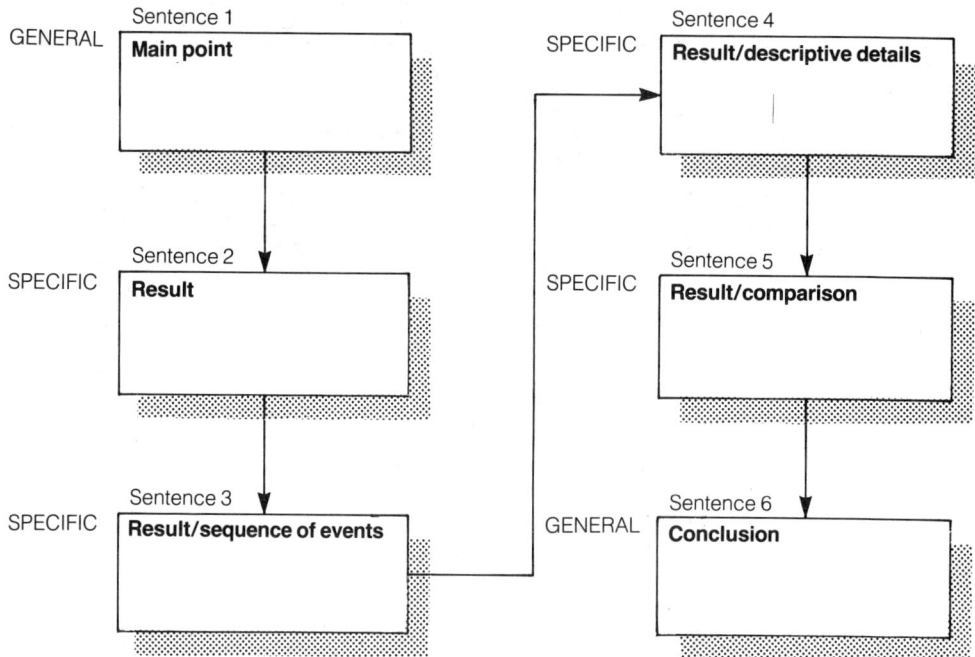

4   Unit One

2 The next diagram shows you one interpretation of how the eruption occurred. You have to write a paragraph explaining this. In groups discuss what the main and supporting points will be. Then jot down an outline for your paragraph with the main point at the beginning. This can be in the form of a diagram like the one you have just filled in. You need only use the information you feel is necessary to support your main point.

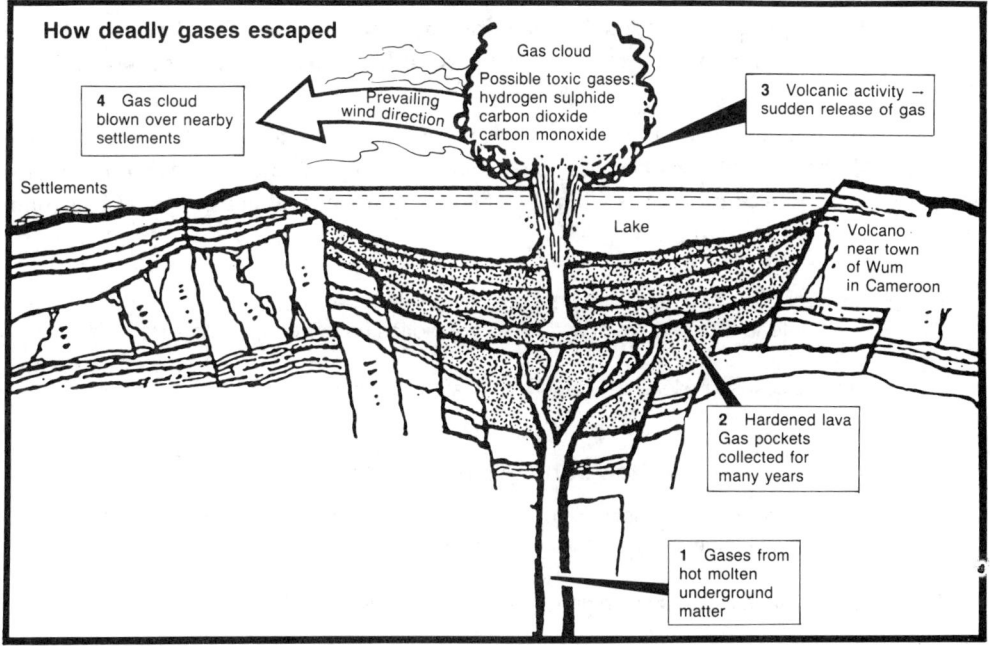

3 Individually write a paragraph following your group's outline.

4 Exchange your text with somebody from another group. Find the main point of the paragraph. Are all the supporting points relevant to the main point and in a good order? Suggest changes to improve your partner's paragraph. Note any suggestions for improving your own. (In Appendix One you can see an example of how you might mark a paragraph in order to indicate how it could be improved.)

5 Bearing in mind the comments made, rewrite your own paragraph making improvements where necessary.

TASK THREE

DEVELOPING EACH PARAGRAPH WITHIN A TEXT

Here you can practise what you have learnt so far by developing the main point of each paragraph in a complete text. As you do this, think about how they develop the central theme of the text. (The development of the central theme is studied more closely in the next unit.)

1 In groups choose one of the following sentence portions to complete the opening paragraph of the text below. Discuss the reasons for your choice. Notice how in this paragraph the sequence of ideas is from specific details to general main point. (This main point is the central theme of this text.)

    (a) . . . but such diseases have since become much more serious.
    (b) . . . but bacteria that once succumbed to antibiotics have evolved into strains that resist these drugs.
    (c) . . . but doctors are no longer sure how to treat these diseases.

A New Form of Drug Abuse

With the introduction of antibiotics four decades ago, a host of dreaded infectious diseases – from scarlet fever to syphillis – lost their power to disfigure, cripple and kill. . .
. . .
The reason for this is indiscriminate use of the 'miracle drugs' over the years.

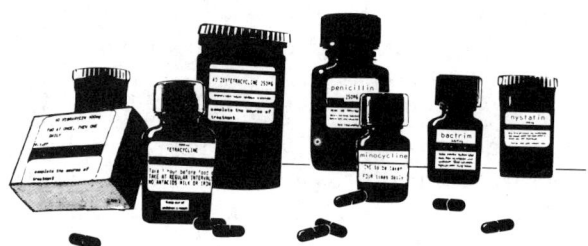

2 Here are some notes for the second paragraph. Write the main point of the paragraph and develop it by writing a suitable sequence of supporting points.

    (a) Last week 150 scientists from 26 countries met. Subject: ways to control global drug abuse.
    (b) Global drug abuse takes form of:
        (i) Antibiotics dispensed without prescription, especially in Third World countries.
        (ii) Drugs prescribed by doctors even when ineffective.
        (iii) Drugs seeping into food chain (reason: farmers use them in animal feed – help prevent disease and promote growth).

(c) Result: almost all of the once-susceptible bacteria destroyed – new drug-resistant strains.
(d) Consequence: public health problem.

3 Use notes (a) and (b), which follow the next paragraph of the text, to complete it.

Several common bacterial infections have already outgrown the antibiotics designed to cure them. . . . . . . 'If we continue to use antibiotics totally freely,' says Nobel Prize winner Walter Gilbert of Harvard University, 'we can look forward to a period in which 80 to 90% of the infectious strains that arise are resistant.'

(a) Penicillin – originally effective against all strains of *staphylococcus aureus* – now only 10%.
(b) Britain – last decade – drug-resistant infections caused by *E. coli* bacteria risen 500%.

4 Look at the completed text. For each paragraph check that the sequence of main and supporting points is a sensible one and that the relationship between them is obvious. Is the central theme well developed throughout the whole text?

TASK FOUR

UNITY OF IDEAS IN A PARAGRAPH

This task looks more closely at achieving unity of ideas in a paragraph. Only points which relate directly to the main idea should be included. Every supporting point should be fully explained so that its relationship to the main point is as clear as possible.

1 Read the following paragraph, which is the opening paragraph of a student essay entitled 'Should our women do compulsory National Service?' Then, in groups, answer the questions that follow it.

```
Republic is a small state with limited land area and limited
resources. Its only resource is its manpower. It therefore has
to depend on other countries for raw materials and energy
supplies to meet the needs of its fast growing industry. This
industrial development together with its strategic position
and flourishing entrepôt trade make it the envy of its
neighbours. For this reason, Republic is a potential target
for invasion. This is especially so when those countries are
not endowed with natural harbours. Thus the government found
it necessary in 1950 to introduce compulsory National Service
for its young men.
```

(a) Bearing in mind the title of the whole essay, what is the writer's main point in this paragraph?
(b) How many supporting points are introduced? What are they?
(c) Do you think they are all useful for supporting the main point or could some of them be omitted entirely?
(d) Can any of the supporting points be reworded so that they develop the main point more obviously?

2   As a group, rewrite the paragraph so that only supporting points directly relevant to the main point are included. Make sure that each supporting point develops the main point in the clearest way possible.

TASK FIVE

PLANNING AND WRITING AN ARTICLE

In this task you will plan and write an article entitled 'Republic's Working Women'.

1   In groups discuss the following questions and make notes of your answers. Data from Republic's Ministry of Employment have been given to help you answer some of them. You have to use your own ideas for the others.

(a) More women are working nowadays. Why is this so?
(b) What has been the trend in the number of women working in Republic over the last thirty years? (Table A will help you.)

TABLE A
Females in the workforce

Year	Total working population	Total women employed	%
1957	480,000	86,000	18
1966	577,000	133,000	23
1974	858,000	276,000	32
1987	1,365,000	650,000	48

(c) Look at the figures in Table B. Each one shows the percentage of all the women in a particular age group in Republic who are working women. For example, of all the women in Republic aged 20–24, 68% are working. Compare this figure with the others. Which of the figures do you find particularly noteworthy? Why? What general statement can you make about how likely it is that women in different age groups will be working?

TABLE B
Percentage of each age group of the female
population that are working women

Age group	%
15–19	45
20–24	68
25–29	46
30–44	28
45 and over	20

(d) How might you explain the figures you examined in question (c)?
(e) What do you think the implications of these figures are:
   (i) For productivity?
   (ii) For the status and pay of women workers?

2 Individually write a five-paragraph article entitled 'Republic's Working Women'. Use the notes you made on each of the five questions above for the content of each paragraph. Write one or two sentences stating the main point for each paragraph and expand your notes for your supporting points. You can write paragraphs which move from a general statement to specific details or vice versa.

3 Exchange articles with another student in your group and make any suggestions you feel would improve your partner's writing with regard to development of the main point in each paragraph and linking between paragraphs.

4 Then rewrite your article as you think necessary.

TASK SIX

FREE WRITING

Write a paragraph for a travel magazine to accompany this photograph, taken in the Philippines. Write on anything the picture brings to your mind. The original heading obviously focuses on the fact that the boy had prepared for his siesta by taking his pillow along, but you can supply a new heading of your own to reflect your main idea.

A Little Creature Comfort

Copyright 1986 Reuters
All rights reserved

UNIT TWO

INTERACTION IN THE TEXT
THE COMPLETE TEXT

Like a well-developed paragraph, a whole text must be unified and coherent. The main points presented in the paragraphs of the text should all develop and support its central theme. A text is made up of three parts. There is an introduction, which introduces the central theme. This is followed by the body of the text, which presents a series of main points and their supporting points. Finally, there is a conclusion, which grows out of the central theme and the main points, and comments on or evaluates them. As in the paragraph, only points that are directly relevant to the central theme should be included.

TASK ONE

UNITY AND COHERENCE IN A TEXT

This task deals with unity and coherence in a text. It presents two essays on the topic of stereotyping in school textbooks. See how successfully you think they develop and support the central theme.

Read both essays and then, in groups, discuss the points below.

1 Briefly summarise the main point of each paragraph. You may want to underline words in the text which help you identify it.

2 Look at the introductory paragraphs. Given that both essays are meant to be about the stereotypes of women in textbooks, how effective do you find each introduction? Is one a clearer introduction to the central theme than the other? If so, why?

3 Look at the main points you identified in (1) above and see how relevant they are to the argument that is being presented in each essay. Do they all develop and support the central theme of the essay?

4 Look at the last paragraph in each essay. Is it a good conclusion? Does it relate to the argument that is presented throughout? Look at the introduction again and see whether the argument presented as the central theme in the introduction is present in the conclusion.

Essay A*

A survey has recently been conducted of the most widely used elementary school textbooks in a number of developed and developing countries across the world. It reveals that these textbooks generally present a stereotype of girls as passive and dependent creatures whose main role in life is to serve their future husbands and children.

The survey shows that most stories and illustrations presented to elementary school children centre on boys rather than girls and that those boys tend to demonstrate qualities of strength, intelligence, love of adventure, independence and courage. Girls, however, are depicted in passive roles. Usually they are inside a house, often helping with housework or playing with dolls. When boys and girls appear together in a text, the girls are either watching the boys do something or they are helping the boys.

A similar pattern can be seen for the adults. The men appearing in elementary school texts are depicted in various jobs – astronaut, truck driver, policeman, cowboy, scientist, banker – in addition to the role of father. But the overwhelming picture of women that emerges is that of mother and housewife, and, more often than not, of women performing simple but time-consuming chores. It fails completely to reflect the complexities facing the modern housewife, much less the working woman.

Discussing the results of the survey, a leading United States child psychologist pointed out that such female stereotyping has a most undesirable effect on girls. They come to think that their role is solely to serve others. Indeed, by the time most of them finish elementary school, they believe they have only four occupations open to them – to become a nurse, teacher, secretary or mother. Consequently, although they generally have better academic records than boys by the time they reach adolescence, they value academic and scholastic excellence less than boys do. Until writers can break away from sexist stereotypes in their stories, girls will continue to see their future as one that is limited by the roles they are expected to play.

Essay B

With the rise of the Women's Movement it is surprising to discover that many school books read by children are filled with elements of sexual prejudice against women. Numerous books recommended by teachers tend to influence children to think that men are dominant in society, while women are passive. This is, of course, not true in modern society where women hold occupations which were previously the exclusive territory of males.

Women are in fact equal to men. This is not to say that there are no differences between them – there are. However, these are not differences of a hierarchical nature. One is not inferior to the other. The differences are primarily physiological and of no real significance when discussing the social roles of both sexes.

One practical problem is the economic disadvantage that can occur if women are perceived as non-contributors to a society's development. This is particularly crucial in developing countries where qualified manpower is essential to economic growth. If these countries see fifty per cent of their potential workforce as housebound child-rearers then a vital human resource is being wasted.

Many schoolbooks depict women washing clothes, cooking dinner, bargaining in the market and taking children to school. They depict, on the other hand, men working in the

*Adapted from *The Washington Post*.

office, driving a car, travelling around the world, socialising in many and varied situations, relating to a wide range of people and dominating the home.

School is one of the most important agents of socialisation and so the material that is presented in school plays an important role in moulding the students' behaviour and attitudes. If students are constantly presented with the same narrow image of women and their place in society, they cannot be blamed for having discriminatory views about the roles of women and men in society.

Although most people nowadays readily accept the broad notion that women are equal to men, they do not see the many inequalities that still exist. Women must fight just to have the same opportunities that are given to men – for a woman to achieve takes twice as much effort as it does for a man. Therein lies the inequality. The society's treatment of women must change and people must change it. We cannot leave it all up to God – she can't do everything!

TASK TWO

SUPPORTING AND DEVELOPING THE CENTRAL THEME OF A TEXT USING THE MAIN POINTS OF THE PARAGRAPHS

The focus of this task is the way the main points of the various paragraphs of a text support and develop its central theme.

1 Read the following text, from which the introduction has been omitted, and then discuss the questions which follow it with a partner.

Speaking to All the World *

1.

2. English is the almost universal language of science, business and international politics. It might be thought, then, that English will become ever more dominant and will, in effect, become the global language – either the first or second language of every person on the planet. But there's a catch!

3. There could be nationalistic reactions against English. It might well seem to billions of people on Earth that those for whom English is the native language would have an advantage over those for whom it is a learned language; that the English-language heritage in literature and in culture generally would cast all others into the shade.

4. What is the alternative? Interpreters? Whether interpretation is human or computerised, could we trust it? How incredibly easy it would be to make small errors in interpretation and how costly those might be. Can we have a global language other than English? Which? Surely any language other than English would create even louder objections the world over. There are artificial languages, of course. The best known is Esperanto, invented in 1887. It is a very sensible language, very easy to learn, but it is essentially a distillation of the Romance languages and might therefore rouse non-European hostility. Besides, artificial languages seem to lack vitality. After a century there are only about 100,000 speakers of Esperanto. Other artificial languages are even less successful.

5. Yet the problem may well take care of itself. As communications around the world improve, and as more and more common folk may want to talk – not just educated businessmen and scientists – 'lingua terra', a 'language of the world', may arise little by little. English will make up a large part of it, yes; but every other language will add vocabulary, idiom, and grammar. It could end as a fearful construction, with rules all its own bearing no too-clear mark of any one national language. All human beings would have to learn it in addition to their own languages, and none would have an advantage over others by the mere accident of place of birth. Lingua terra could end with a vocabulary, a flexibility, a richness surpassing any other, so that it could develop a mighty literature of its own. It might then, by its mere existence, do more to emphasise the familyhood of humanity than a million sermons on the subject laid end to end.

*Reprinted from *Change!* by Isaac Asimov. Copyright 1983 Hodder & Stoughton and Walter Damtoft.

(a) What is each paragraph about? Underline the sentence(s) which presents the main point of each paragraph.
(b) Are the main points of the paragraphs related to each other? How?
(c) What is the theme that seems to run through the paragraphs? Write one or two sentences that present the central theme of this text.

2 Individually write an introductory paragraph for this text that incorporates the central theme you have written.

3 Exchange your paragraph with your partner. Check that the central theme of the text is clearly introduced. Look at the way this introduction leads to the next paragraph – is the transition well managed?

4 If necessary rewrite your paragraph in the light of your partner's comments.

TASK THREE

ADEQUATE CONCLUSIONS

In this task you have to think about the relationships between parts of a text and the relationship between these parts and the central theme so as to write an adequate conclusion.

1 First read this magazine article, from which the conclusion has been omitted, and complete the diagram that follows it.

Water – Everybody's Problem

Whether trying to live with the depressing spectacle of drought or battling rampaging floods or suffering with a debilitating disease caused by contaminated drinking supplies, people in almost every corner of the world have had their problems with the vagaries of water. Although water covers much of our planet, more than 97% is in the oceans. Another 2% is unusable ice. And much of the remainder is polluted. So much for the supposed abundance! Developed and developing countries alike are now talking about a crisis.

2   What of the future? Will water needs reach a peak? Unhappily, UN experts expect demands to double in the next 25 years. This will coincide with increasing population and industrialisation – and the attendant risk of factory and human wastes further contaminating rivers, lakes and ground water. So, is there any hope of a solution? The answer, fortunately, is that the problem is being tackled.

3   Specialists in many countries are developing methods to improve supply and conservation and protect quality, and a number of ambitious programmes have been undertaken. Good forecasting – including predictions of snow, rain, river levels and soil loss – can help scientists head off, or at least cope with, floods. Canals can ease one of the major water-related problems: drought. With something like three-quarters of the world's fresh water tied up as ice, plans to drag icebergs to drought areas have been around for a long time; attempts to overcome the drawbacks – a great deal of energy would be needed to tow the ice and pump the water inland, and the ice might melt before reaching its destination – are still being made. In addition, research into desalting sea-water continues with new and improving desalting methods although no method can yet promise truly low-cost fresh water. Fossil water – underground water dating back to the ice age – could be drilled for in some areas but supplies are non-renewable. Work continues in all these areas. It is obvious that a lot of time, money and research is going into finding solutions for some of the problems.

4   However, worldwide, the ugly fact remains that something like 250 million new cases of water-borne diseases are discovered every year – and 25,000 people die from them every day. Pollution continues to plague us – all of us. 'Even as the rain falls,' says Russell W. Peterson, former chairman of the US Council on Environmental Quality, 'it scours pollutants from the air. In fact, nearly all the pollutants the people of the world discharge into the air end up in our water systems.' So, whether tainted by industrial waste, sewage or other pollution, unreliable water supplies frequently create breeding grounds for deadly water-borne diseases when safeguards and purification are inadequate.

Central theme of text (Write complete sentence(s))

Structure of text (Write in note form)

The facts → Question

Expected future problems → Question

Question → The problem is being tackled / Evaluation of projects

→ One further problem

→ ?.

2 Conclusions are not restricted to the end of a text. In both paragraphs two and three of this article, the writer has drawn conclusions based on the preceding content of the paragraph. Can you identify each of these conclusions?

3 What might an appropriate final conclusion for this text include? Working in small groups, make notes of points you feel would be relevant. Justify your points by indicating in the columns of the table below how and where they relate to the rest of the text and its central theme. An example of such a point is given in the table.

Content of conclusion	Has the point been referred to in the text? YES/NO	Indicate in which paragraph of text	Does the point clearly connect to central theme? YES/NO
Summary of water related problems (droughts, floods, contamination)	YES	1,2,3,4	YES

4 Individually, arrange your group's points into the sequence you think best and write the conclusion to this article.

5 Read each other's conclusions. Check that the sequence of ideas is a good one and that the central theme of the entire text is adequately rounded off.

6 Rewrite your paragraph if necessary.

TASK FOUR

'INTERMEDIATE' CONCLUSIONS

In Task Three you considered the relation between text and final conclusion. You also saw how conclusions may appear towards the end of paragraphs within a written text as well as at the end of it. Such conclusions, referred to here as 'intermediate' conclusions, are also drawn from points previously made by the writer. As a result, they are usually important sentences within the text. Accordingly, care must be taken to ensure that:

(a) any 'intermediate' conclusion relates adequately to the content that precedes it, and
(b) the central theme of the text is developed and supported by both the 'intermediate' conclusion(s) and the final conclusion(s).

Here you will be writing the body of a text with an 'intermediate' conclusion and choosing an appropriate final conclusion for the text.

1 Read the following introduction to a newspaper article and identify the central theme. State this idea in a sentence. Do your classmates agree with you?

Promoting Child Development

It is generally accepted that some knowledge of the stages of physical and mental development that children go through is essential in raising children. This is certainly important during their pre-school and kindergarten years. Educational psychologists have pointed out one way of promoting the healthy development of the three to five year old child. They suggest that parents should cater to and reinforce the developmental characteristics their children exhibit. To illustrate how parents might go about this, they offer the example of selecting reading material for children.

2 Prepare to continue writing the text by first filling each blank in the following table with one item chosen from the appropriate list below it. List A describes some types of book. List B gives titles of books which are examples of these types. Make sure the suggested type of book you choose relates closely to the given 'Characteristics of children' and thus to the central theme of the text.

Choosing Books for Children of Pre-school and Kindergarten Age

Characteristics of children	Suggested type of book	Example
They display rapid development of language ability. They are very active, with short attention spans. They are very egocentric: they see themselves as the centre of the world. They are beginning to make simple value judgements.		

List A

(a) Books which portray characters with which the child can readily identify: they help the child to understand who he is in relation to others.

(b) Books which are considered classics and are often passed down from one generation to another.

(c) Books which encourage short-duration participation through naming, touching and pointing activities.

(d) Books which present interesting, repetitive and enjoyable rhymes, words and phrases.

(e) Books which come with audio tape cassettes to which the child can listen while looking at the book.

(f) Books which present stories involving poetic justice and happy endings.

List B

1. *Circles, Triangles, and Squares*
In this book differently sized shapes of different colours are presented for identification.

2. *The Tale of Peter Rabbit*
This is a popular story where the good characters are rewarded while the naughty are punished.

3. *Me I See*
This book helps young children to consider how each child is an individual, different from other children.

4. *Grimm's Fairy Tales*
These traditional European folk tales were collected around the year 1850.

5. *Mother Goose*
These stories and poems make playful use of language.

6. *Goldilocks*
This is a popular story about a little girl's encounter with three bears, presented through book and audio tape.

3 Decide how the information in your completed table can be used to develop the central theme. Write a paragraph based on the table to continue from the introduction and form the main body of the text. You should include an appropriate 'intermediate' conclusion which specifically comments on the points presented in this paragraph. This can refer to the ease with which the content of books can be related to children's developmental characteristics.

4 Choose the most appropriate conclusion for the text you have written from the three given below. Discuss the reasons for your choice.

1 The period of development undergone by three- to five-year-old children is marked by rapid physical and psychological growth. However, awareness of the evolving developmental characteristics of the child will enable parents to enjoy this fascinating process. It will also make parenting that much easier.

2 Just as with books, it should be equally easy to relate toys, games, and even group activities to the developmental characteristics of young children. If the experts are right, then by carefully choosing activities which relate to the stage of development, we have at least one more way of providing children with a sound upbringing.

3 Thus parents who want to develop a positive attitude to reading in their child should not find it difficult. By relating the developmental characteristics of the child to the content of the books he is given to read, parents can ensure that he will be interested in the book and in addition be well on the way to reading competence.

5 Look carefully at your complete text. Has the central theme been adequately developed, supported and concluded?

TASK FIVE

RELATING A CENTRAL THEME, 'INTERMEDIATE' CONCLUSIONS AND FINAL CONCLUSION

In this lesson you will have further practice relating the central theme, the 'intermediate' conclusion(s) and final conclusion(s) in a text.

The three case studies given below show typical examples of how some employees are promoted and how they perform their duties after promotion. The phenomenon illustrated in the case studies has been referred to as the 'Peter Principle'.*

*Reprinted from *The Peter Principle* by Laurens J. Peter and Raymond Hull. Copyright 1969 Souvenir Press.

1 Read the following case studies.

A

Municipal Government File, Case No. 17

J.S. Minion was a maintenance foreman in the Public Works department of Excelsior City. He was a favourite of the senior officials at City Hall. They all praised his unfailing affability.

'I like Minion,' said the Superintendent of Works. 'He has good judgement and is always pleasant and agreeable.'

This behaviour was appropriate for Minion's position: he was not supposed to make policy, so he had no need to disagree with his superiors.

The Superintendent of Works retired and Minion succeeded him. Minion continued to agree with everyone. He passed on to his foreman every suggestion that came from above. The resulting conflicts in policy, and the continual changing of plans, soon demoralised the department. Complaints poured in from the Mayor and other officials, from taxpayers and from the maintenance workers' union. The Maintenance Department regularly exceeds its budget, yet fails to fulfil its programme of work.

Minion still says 'Yes' to everyone, and carries messages briskly back and forth between his superiors and his subordinates.

B

Service Industries File, Case No. 3

E. Tinker was exceptionally zealous and intelligent as an apprentice at G. Reece Auto Repair Inc., and soon rose to journeyman mechanic. In this job he showed outstanding ability in diagnosing obscure faults, and endless patience in correcting them. He was promoted to foreman of the repair shop.

But here his love of things mechanical and his perfectionism became liabilities. He will undertake any job that he thinks looks interesting, no matter how busy the shop may be. 'We'll work it in somehow,' he says.

He will not let a job go until he is fully satisfied with it.

He meddles constantly. He is seldom to be found at his desk. He is usually up to his elbows in a dismantled motor: and while the man who should be doing the work stands watching, other workmen sit around waiting to be assigned new tasks. As a result the shop is always overcrowded with work, always in a muddle, and delivery times are often missed.

Tinker cannot understand that the average customer cares little about perfection – he wants his car back on time! He cannot understand that most of his men are less interested in motors than in their pay cheques. So Tinker cannot get on with his customers or with his subordinates.

C

**Education file
Case No. 31**

Miss Totland, who had been a competent student and an outstanding primary teacher, was promoted to primary supervisor. She now has to teach, not children, but teachers. Yet she still uses the techniques which worked so well with small children.

Addressing teachers, singly or in groups, she speaks slowly and distinctly. She uses mostly words of one or two syllables. She explains each point several times in different ways, to be sure it is understood. She always wears a bright smile.

Teachers dislike what they call her false cheerfulness and her patronising attitude. Their resentment is so sharp that, instead of trying to carry out her suggestions, they spend much time devising excuses for not doing what she recommends.

2 Discuss the three case studies in groups. Write down one or two sentences to answer each of these questions.

(a) Why were these three employees promoted?
(b) How effective were they after promotion? Why was this so?
(c) How do these three case studies explain incompetence at higher levels of the workforce?
(d) The principle that is said to be operating in case studies like these is known as the 'Peter Principle'. How would you describe it?

3 Now, individually:

(a) Write the introduction to a text entitled 'The Peter Principle'. The main body of your text will continue with the case studies given above. You do not need to rewrite them.
(b) In the main body of your text, provide an 'intermediate' conclusion for each case study, relating each one to the central theme you have presented in your introduction.
(c) Write a conclusion which relates to and follows from the content of the case studies and their 'intermediate' conclusions and the central theme of your text.

4 Look at some of your classmates' texts with these questions in mind:

(a) What is the central theme?
(b) Are the 'intermediate' and final conclusions appropriately drawn and do they relate well to the central theme?

TASK SIX

REPORT-WRITING: RELATION OF INTRODUCTION, SUPPORTING PARAGRAPHS AND CONCLUSION TO CENTRAL THEME

Your analysis of the data given here will provide you with the content for a report on a survey on divorce in Republic. Writing the report will give you more practice in relating the introduction, the paragraphs making up the main body of the text and the conclusion to the central theme.

1 Read the following information and think about possible central themes for your report.

Background
The number of women in Republic who end their marriages has been rising for the past two decades. However, traditional reasons for divorce, e.g. adultery, infertility, physical cruelty and desertion on the part of the husband, have not been cited as grounds for proceedings to a much greater extent than before. Indeed, many of the women now seeking divorce appear from the outside to lead very satisfying lives. What, then, is responsible for the increase? To answer this a questionnaire was designed to try to identify possible reasons why women choose to end their marriages.

The Study
The questionnaire was first administered to a sample of 300 women who were either seeking divorce or who had already been successful in obtaining one. Next, a control group of 500 married women, comparable to those in the sample group in age, race, income, place of residence prior to divorce, religious affiliations and husband's occupational status were selected and given the same questionnaire.

2 In groups, study the questionnaire to identify possible reasons for women choosing to end their marriages. The following steps should help you in interpreting the data.

(a) Group together those questions which you feel are directed towards a common area. State what these areas are.
(b) Compare your classification with those of other groups in your class. Make any revisions you feel are appropriate to your classification.
(c) Take each area in turn and compare the responses of the divorced and the married women noting similarities and differences. You should be able to make generalisations from them about factors which affect the success of a marriage. Many of these generalisations can be used as the main points in the body of your report. Your choice of main points should follow from and support your selection of a central theme. Where the responses from the two groups are similar, what conclusion can you draw about the effect of this factor on the marriage? Where the responses are very different, what conclusions do they suggest?

The Questionnaire and Responses

	Divorced			Married		
	Yes %	No %	NA %	Yes %	No %	NA %
1. Do you have children?	82	18	–	85	15	–
(If response to 1 is 'Yes')						
A. Do your children still live at home?/Did they live at home when divorce proceedings began?	27	55	18	34	51	15
B. Did/Do you have the main responsibility for their discipline?	61	21	18	45	40	15
C. All things considered, have they 'turned out' well?	45	37	18	45	40	15
D. Have you ever had a serious argument with your parents or in-laws on the children's upbringing?	36	46	18	32	52	16
2. Was/Is your marriage characterised by financial difficulties?	12	88	–	15	85	–
3. Did/Do you feel ignored by your husband?	72	28	–	10	90	–
4. Do you think you have 'achieved' in life so far?	23	77	–	54	46	–
5. Did/Do you feel your husband took/takes too little time to sit down and talk things out?	81	19	–	51	49	–
6. Do you feel that much of your life has been without purpose?	38	62	–	11	89	–
7. Did/Does your husband regard you as inferior to himself?	84	16	–	14	86	–
8. Did your parents separate or divorce?	22	78	–	24	76	–
9. Was/Is your husband too absorbed in his work?	63	37	–	25	75	–
10. Do you think your life could be *much* better than it has been?	75	25	–	38	62	–
11. Did/Does your mother work outside the home?	35	65	–	21	79	–
A. After her marriage but before the birth of her first child?	29	71	–	16	84	–
B. After the birth(s) of her child(ren)?	25	75	–	9	91	–
C. After her children started school?	31	69	–	11	89	–
D. After they left home?	33	67	–	12	88	–
12. Have you had enough education to do what you want?	29	71	–	40	60	–

	Divorced			Married		
	Yes %	No %	NA %	Yes %	No %	NA %
13. Did you complete primary school?	97	3	–	95	5	–
A. Did you complete high school?	71	29	–	60	40	–
B. Did you complete college/university?	45	55	–	35	65	–
14. Do you consider yourself to be of above average intelligence?	70	30	–	55	45	–
15. Did you regard yourself as popular when you were younger?	64	36	–	69	31	–
16. Are you satisfied on the whole with your present employment status?	32	68	–	55	45	–
17. Would you work if you had enough money to live comfortably without working?	71	29	–	34	66	–
18. Is life for single people less rewarding than it is for married people?	26	74	–	83	17	–
19. Did/Do your family responsibilities leave you with no time for yourself?	81	19	–	57	43	–

3 Individually, write a report entitled 'Divorce in Republic'.

4 Before handing in your report, exchange texts with another student. Can you make any suggestions about how your partner could improve the interaction of main and supporting points in each paragraph and the way they contribute to the central theme?

TASK SEVEN

WRITING A COMPLETE TEXT WITH INTRODUCTION, BODY AND FINAL CONCLUSION

In this task you have to use your own ideas to write a complete text with an introduction, body and final conclusion.

You are to contribute to helping new students in your institution. This means introducing a student orientation programme at the beginning of each course to help new students with problems they are likely to have in their new environment.

1   In small groups, discuss:

(a) What problems and needs new students are likely to have.
(b) What activities can be introduced to help them with these problems and needs.

2   Making use of the ideas discussed in (1), individually write a leaflet to inform your fellow students of your proposals. Your leaflet should include:

(a) An introduction stating your proposal and the reasons for it and informing students that you need their support.
(b) A main body describing the activities that can be introduced and pointing out how these can help new students.
(c) A conclusion in which you emphasise the importance and usefulness of such a programme and urge your fellow students to help in organising it.

UNIT THREE

INTERACTION WITH THE READER
MEETING THE NEEDS OF THE READER

It is important when writing to bear in mind who the reader will be and what information, if any, he can be expected to have about the subject. This helps the writer decide what information needs to be supplied in the text. Although it is not always possible to give definite answers to these questions, it is always necessary to make some assumptions. The purpose of writing must also be identified so as to decide what information is relevant. Very often, appropriate information is not provided: a writer gives either too little, too much or the wrong information. In addition, it is important to help the reader by making sure that every new idea is fully developed and the links between ideas are made explicit.

TASK ONE

A RESPONSE: THE SELECTION OF APPROPRIATE INFORMATION FROM ONE TEXT TO BE INCORPORATED IN ANOTHER

Sometimes a text is written in response to another text or a situation of which the reader may not be aware. To enable the reader to follow the new text, the writer must include information appropriate to his purpose from the original text or situation. In this letter, written to the editor of a newspaper for publication in the letters column, you can see how appropriate information is selected and incorporated in a new text.

1   Read the letter and in groups answer the questions which follow it.

Dear Editor

I refer to the letter of 14 September – 'For a Few Dollars More' – by Expatriate, in which the writer complains about the work attitude of our local employees. However, from reading the letter, it appears to me that the problem Expatriate faces is not one of work attitude on the part of local employees but one of management style on the part of the international company of which he is the chief executive. It is common knowledge that working conditions and management style are instrumental in forging employees' attitude. To what extent is the problem Expatriate complains of in his employees something of his own making? It would not be a bad idea for Expatriate to examine his own management style and the working conditions he provides his employees with before accusing the local employees so readily.

Expatriate claims that 'for a few dollars more' employees change jobs without hesitation. The question I would like to ask is whether he has examined the wage structure in his company and compared it with that of other firms within the same industry and in the local employment market as a whole.

As to his point that local employees are unwilling to admit mistakes and accept criticism, it is important to ask if his company provides the kind of atmosphere which promotes mutual trust and respect among its employees, thereby encouraging the admission of mistakes and acceptance of criticism. It is unrealistic to expect employees to give their best when they know the negative and prejudiced opinion their chief executive has of them, an opinion which is only too obvious from the letter he has written.

In the opinion of Expatriate, local employees are also guilty of rudeness and abruptness. Is it possible that in a country like ours where English is a second language, what appears to be rudeness and abruptness may be the result of inadequate command of the language? Expatriate does not seem to be aware that in cross-cultural communication, it is important to adopt an understanding attitude and to allow certain flexibility in the use of a language which is not the speaker's mother-tongue.

It is indeed ironic that a person who is capable of such an elaborate analysis of the many shortcomings of our local employees is at the same time completely blind to the obvious root of the problem. At least he indicates he still harbours confidence in the local worker. So do I.

Local Worker

(a) Who are the likely readers of this letter? Can we assume that they have read the letter of 14 September to which the present letter refers?
(b) What essential information from the original letter has Local Worker included in his letter so that the reader will be able to understand his reply? Can you tell the content of Expatriate's letter from reading Local Worker's reply?
  (i) What is Expatriate's official capacity in his company? Why is it important for the reader to know this?
  (ii) Underline the sentences which refer to the general content of the earlier letter.
  (iii) List the specific points from Expatriate's letter to which Local Worker refers.

TASK TWO

THE IDENTIFICATION OF INFORMATION NEEDED BY THE READER

Here is a piece of writing that does not consider the information that the reader may need. You will be asked to write a similar passage which does provide the necessary information.

The following passage was written by a student after hearing a story. She was asked to write down her feelings about the characters, based on their actions, for a reader who had *not* heard the story. The original story is reproduced in Appendix Two.

```
Abigail was in love with Gregory. They lived on opposite shores of
a river. Every day Abigail would visit Gregory by crossing the
bridge that spanned the river. One day the bridge was destroyed by
a storm. Although she was a good swimmer she could not swim across
the river because there were alligators in it. I feel sympathetic
towards Abigail who was so much in love with Gregory that she was
willing to give gold to Sinbad so that she could meet Gregory. She
is to be sympathised with because Gregory, blinded by anger,
treated her badly. But I also feel sympathetic towards Gregory
because he was badly beaten by Simon. Although Gregory acted
unreasonably and thoughtlessly, Simon should not have beaten him
up so badly for I think Gregory's action was understandable in the
circumstances. I do not like Ivan because he showed no sympathy
for Abigail when she told him her problem. I dislike Simon because
he acted without thinking. As for Sinbad he is to be despised
because he exploited the situation poor Abigail was in to satisfy
his greed.
```

1 Discuss this passage in a small group and write down any questions you want to ask about this story. In other words, what is not explained in the passage which you feel needs clarification?

2 Now your teacher will read you the original story. After hearing it, choose one character and write your feelings about him/her for a reader who has not heard the story. Include sufficient information from the story by providing a brief summary of the relevant points at the beginning to show your reader why you feel this way about the character. Make sure your reader will have no unanswered questions similar to those you asked in (1).

3 Before you hand in your passage to your teacher, find someone to read it who has not heard the story. See if he or she has any questions to ask you about your text.

TASK THREE

THE ADEQUATE DEVELOPMENT OF IDEAS TO BE CLEARLY EXPRESSED AND EXPLICITLY LINKED

It is important to make sure that your reader can easily understand the information you give him. Every idea should be adequately developed and clearly expressed and the links between ideas should be explicit. Your reader should never have to try to read your mind or to make links by himself. If he does, he could reach the wrong conclusions. He will certainly find your text difficult to read if he has to keep guessing at your meaning.

The excerpts below are examples of students' writing which is difficult for the reader to follow because he has to draw his own conclusions about what the writer means. This is either because an idea is not adequately developed or because the link between ideas is not specified.

1 In groups, read the excerpts and discuss the questions that follow them.

> **A** Young minds are easily influenced by fascinating things. Therefore censorship is a must to avoid having too many unwanted babies.

(a) Do you know exactly what the writer means by 'fascinating things'? What do you think he means?
(b) Has the writer explained how young people are adversely affected by fascinating things?
In what ways do you think they might be influenced?
(c) Is the relationship between censored materials and fewer unwanted babies made clear? How would censorship avoid having too many unwanted babies?

> **B** One tenth of the world's population is living in hunger. Therefore many countries with large populations have attempted either by persuasion or force to curb their population growth. Let me cite as an example China, the most highly populated country in the world. It is desperately trying to decrease its birth rate.

Has the writer stated explicitly what she thinks is the relationship between hunger and countries with large populations? What do you think the connection is? Could there be more than one interpretation?

> **C** Economic progress since independence has been phenomenal. The affluence enjoyed by Republic, however, is not without its consequences. With the deluge of new ideas from films, books, television programmes, magazines and so on, traditional values are being influenced, shaped and altered.

Has the writer explained how the deluge of new ideas is a consequence of affluence? Why do you think this is so?

2 Using the ideas you came up with in your discussion, individually rewrite each excerpt making sure that you explain all the ideas fully and show the relationships between ideas clearly. Do not leave your reader to guess at the significance of an idea as you had to do when you read the excerpts.

Task Three

TASK FOUR

GIVING DIRECTIONS: MAKING ADEQUATE ASSUMPTIONS

To decide what information to supply in any piece of writing, you have to consider how much your reader already knows about your subject. In this task you have to write two different sets of directions for two people with different knowledge about the location in question. You will see how your selection of information is controlled by the knowledge you assume your reader to have.

1 Working in pairs, discuss how you would give directions to a location in your institution or in its vicinity with your classroom as the starting point. Consider how these directions would differ for:

- **Reader A** A fellow student who has never been to the designated place but is familiar with the area – with landmarks, for example.
- **Reader B** A tourist or visitor who is not familiar with your surroundings.

2 Individually write two sets of directions which take into account the different needs of these two readers.

3 Exchange your two sets of directions with your partner. Look at what he or she has written to see:

(a) What information has been given to both Reader A and Reader B and what information to only one reader.
(b) Which text is longer. Why is this?
(c) Whether any of the directions are hard to understand. If so, why is this?

4 Now compare your partner's two sets of directions with your own. Together discuss the following questions:

(a) Have you both included the same points for Reader A? If not, decide which points should be included.
(b) What about for Reader B? Again, see if you have both included the same points. If not, choose those that should be included.
(c) Has one of you written instructions which are easier to follow? If so, can you explain why this is?

5 Based on your discussion in (4), together write a revised version of each set of directions. Use the best parts of each person's writing or change anything you feel necessary to ensure your reader's success in finding the location.

TASK FIVE

INCORPORATING NECESSARY BACKGROUND INFORMATION

This task again focuses on the importance of incorporating necessary background information into your text to ensure that your reader can understand what you write.

Your class will be divided into two parts and each will be given a separate writing task to do, either A or B below. After you have written your text you will read the text of a student who did the other task to see if your needs as a reader have been met.

A THE ADMINISTRATIVE ASSISTANT

A.1 Study the following information.

The situation:

The Students' Union of Republic University needs a full-time administrative assistant.

The advertisement:

The Republic University Students' Union invites applications for the post of
Administrative Assistant

Duties involved include:
- Composing and typing correspondence
- Meeting the public, especially students
- Maintaining correspondence and financial records
- Attending meetings and representing the union in all business matters
- Working without direct supervision

Qualifications preferred include:
- Two years' experience in a similar position
- BA degree in Business Administration or related field
- Some experience with basic accounting practices
- Typing ability of at least 50 wpm
- Bilingual in Republicanese/English

Salary will be commensurate with qualifications and experience. Attractive conditions of service and fringe benefits will be offered to the successful applicant. Send your curriculum vitae and letter of application to:

RUSU
Republic University
10 Egdir Road
Republic 1105

The shortlist:

Applicant X
- Male, age 28.
- BA degree in Business Administration.
- Worked four years in consumer affairs office as assistant to and under the close supervision of the Managing Director.
- Duties performed include writing of news release and consumer information bulletins, researching product quality reports and studies of advertising techniques.
- First language: Republicanese; moderate command of English.
- Types 25 wpm.

Applicant Y
- Female, age 32.
- BA degree in Arts (Sociology).
- Completed accountancy certificate in London.
- Has three years' experience running a two-person regional office for an international social welfare agency (supervisor was located in Geneva).
- Duties performed include maintaining financial records, writing reports on funding of local social welfare institutions, dealing with public – especially local social agency representatives, news media staff and welfare recipients.
- Speaks and writes Republicanese and English fluently.
- Types 55 wpm.

A.2 In groups evaluate the suitability of each applicant on the shortlist by comparing the descriptions of them with the duties and qualifications described in the advertisement – choose the applicant you think best meets the requirements specified.

A.3 Individually write an account explaining how and why your group reached its decision. You should include sufficient information for your account to be read and understood by another student who knows *nothing* of the background to your task. You should fully justify your choice with reference to the descriptions of the applicants and the advertisement for the post.

A.4 Exchange texts with a student who did B. Read your partner's account and then write your answers to the following questions. If the account has successfully taken the reader's needs into consideration you should have no difficulty answering the questions.

(a) What was the group's task?
(b) What scheme was used to evaluate the two teams of workers?
(c) In what areas was each team evaluated and how many points were awarded to each team for each area?
(d) What are the principal differences between the two teams of workers?
(e) Has enough background and/or supporting information been supplied for you to understand the text? Describe any area of information you feel is lacking.
(f) Do you feel the best team has been chosen? (Has the choice been justified?) Write down any questions/doubts you have about the choice of team.

A.5 Give your written answers to your partner and check his/her comments against your text. Discuss your findings with each other.

A.6 Rewrite your text making any changes you feel are necessary following your partner's evaluation.

B THE TEAMWORK AWARD

B.1 Study the following information.

The situation:

> Two teams of factory workers are competing for an award for teamwork. Each team was extensively interviewed and evaluated by a panel of industrial psychologists and the following team profiles were drawn up. No scores for the five areas of assessment have been awarded yet.

The team profiles:

```
1. Mutual Trust
Team A
This team are friendly with each other on and off the job and
have been working with each other for a number of years.  They
appear to trust each other implicitly and do not interfere
with each other's performance of duties.  The supervisor
appears confident that all of his workers are responsible and
gives them considerable freedom to act independently on their
work assignments.
Team B
This team has a reputation for working as a cohesive group
despite the fact that there has been some turnover in the
staff. The workers don't interact socially but seem to make an
effort to trust each other at work.  The supervisor, however,
only fully trusts those workers who have been on the job with
him for a longer period of time.  Some of the workers have
noted this with some resentment.

2. Cooperation
Team A
The members of this team appear to work somewhat independently
of each other and sometimes end up doing something on their
own which might better be done through cooperative efforts.
Team B
The members of this team appear to work well together. Most of
the time, a team member who is good at performing a particular
task will help someone who is less familiar with it.  Because
of this tendency,  their supervisor has identified areas of
expertise for each worker and makes sure that this information
is circulated among the staff and kept current. The supervisor
directs this cooperation but the team members also cooperate
on their own initiative.
```

3. Communication
Team A
This team prides itself on the openness with which the members communicate with one another but this sharing is of a personal and social nature and is rarely job-related. The supervisor encourages them to talk to him regarding personal matters.
Team B
Team members readily communicate with one another but this communication is limited to setting up cooperative efforts. Shared knowledge of policies, individual concerns, and supervisor-employee dialogue are somewhat limited and not encouraged by the supervisor.

4. Commitment
Team A
This team readily displays enthusiasm for achieving their goals. They arrive punctually for work, readily work extra hours and make little use of sick leave. Some take work home with them to do, when it is appropriate to do so.
Team B
This team verbally express a high degree of enthusiasm for their work and meeting their goals but this is not always supported by every member's work record. A few team members overstay their break periods or arrive a little late for work every day. Most, however, appear to be honestly committed to their jobs and do not exhibit such behaviour.

5. Team Problem Solving
Team A
Individual team members are quite good at identifying problems and the supervisor assigns tasks to help in resolving them. These problems are addressed by individuals with little effort made to coordinate efforts. Fortunately, the individuals are competent in what they do but there is some question of how the team would respond to a major crisis that required a coordinated group effort to tackle it successfully.
Team B
This team resolves conflicts and problems by cooperatively addressing them with or without the supervisor directing their efforts. The workers understand the need to solve problems that come up and show individual initiative in this regard.

B.2 In groups evaluate the profiles of the two teams. Give each team a score for each of the five areas of assessment using the guidelines given for scoring and interpretation. Choose the team you think should receive the award for teamwork.

Guidelines for Scoring and Interpretation

5 = excellent teamwork
4 = above average teamwork
3 = average teamwork
2 = fair teamwork
1 = poor teamwork

To interpret the score, add the points for all five areas of assessment:

21–25 points = superior teamwork
15–20 points = competent teamwork but some weaknesses are present
10–14 points = deficient teamwork with major problems apparent
Less than 10 points = little or no evidence of teamwork

B.3 Individually write an account explaining how and why your group reached its decision. You should include sufficient information for your account to be read and understood by another student who knows *nothing* of the background to your task. You should fully justify your choice with reference to the number of points awarded to each team in each area and the reason for the points awarded.

B.4 Exchange texts with a student who did A. Read your partner's account and then write your answers to the following questions. If the account has successfully taken the reader's needs into consideration, you should have no difficulty answering the questions.

(a) What was the group's task?
(b) What are the primary duties of the position being recruited for?
(c) What are the preferred qualifications of the applicants?
(d) What are the shortcomings of Applicant X with regard to his qualifications for the job? Applicant Y?
(e) Has enough background and/or supporting information been supplied for you to understand the text? Describe any area of information you feel is lacking.
(f) Do you feel the best applicant has been chosen? (Has the choice been justified?) Write down any questions/doubts you have about the choice of administrative assistant.

B.5 Give your written answers to your partner and check his/her comments against your text. Discuss your findings with each other.

B.6 Rewrite your text making any changes you feel are necessary following your partner's evaluation.

TASK SIX

CONSIDERING THE PURPOSE IN WRITING

For this task it is very important to consider carefully your reader and your purpose in writing. This will help you to decide what to include in your text to meet the reader's needs and achieve the specified goal.

The pictures that follow were taken at the scene of a crime. You have to use them to write a report for the police to help them in their investigation of the incident. As the police depend entirely on your report to help them trace and identify the robber, adequate detail is required to meet their needs.

1 In small groups examine the pictures closely and decide on your account of the incident. List all the details you think useful to the police under the following major headings with any subheadings you feel appropriate (e.g. physical features of the robber, attire of the robber, etc.):

> When
> Where } the incident happened.
> How
> The robber and his accomplice (if any).
> The vehicle used for the crime.

When you have done this you have the outline for your report.

2 Compare your outline with another group's to:

(a) Add items to your list to make it as full as possible.
(b) Remove items from your list that are not relevant to your purpose or useful to your reader.

3 Write your report individually using the outline you have drawn up in your group.

4 Return to your group and compare texts. Choose the most useful one to submit to the police.

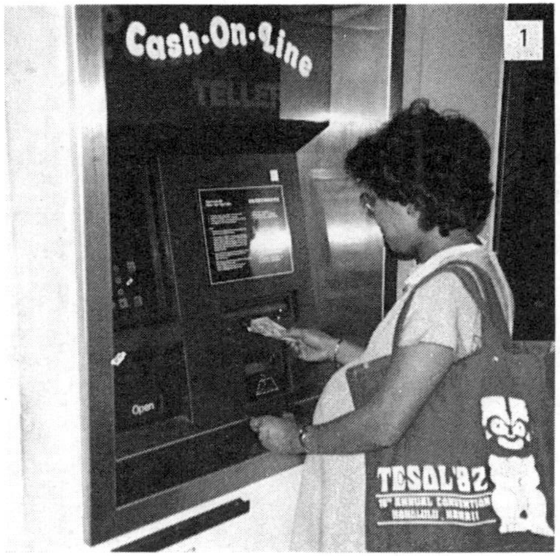
1
Cash-On-Line
TESOL'82

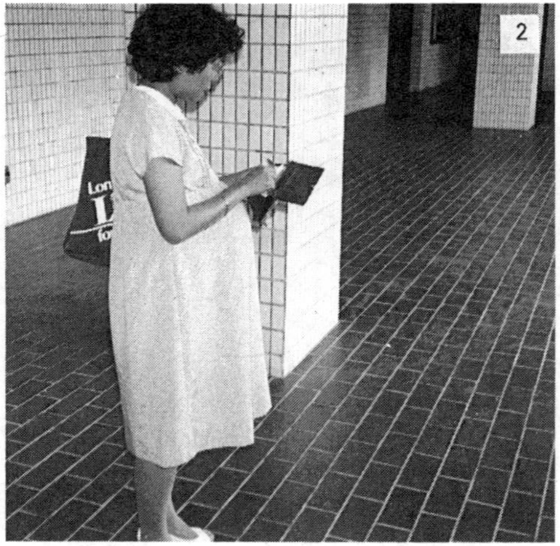
2

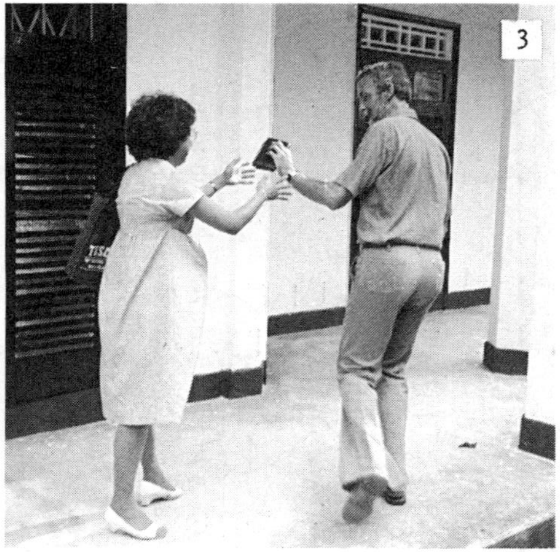
3

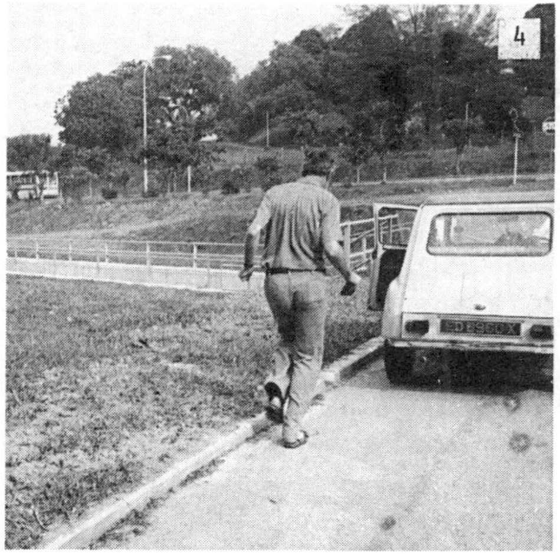
4

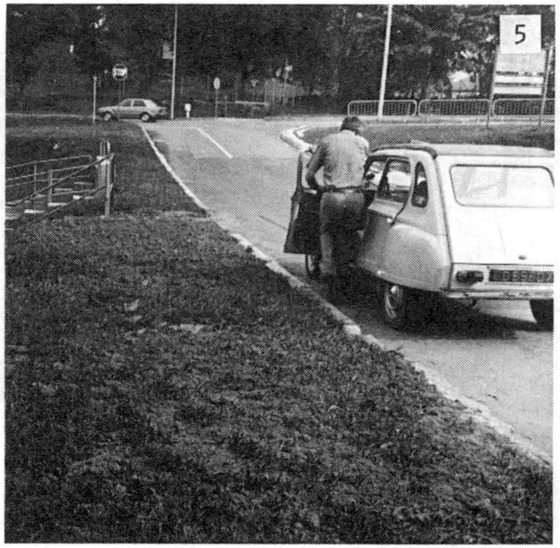
5

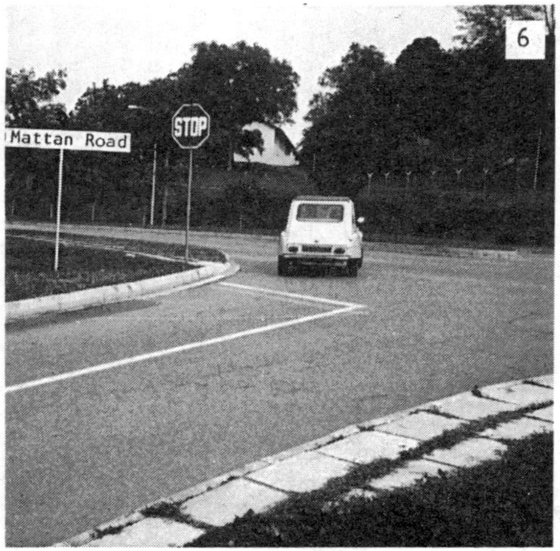
6
Mattan Road
STOP

TASK SEVEN

WRITING A REVIEW

This task requires you to apply what you have learned in this unit about how consideration for the needs of your reader and the purpose of your writing should determine what you say and how you say it in a piece of writing.

1 Write a review of a television programme or a film you have seen or a book you have read recently for a student newspaper or magazine. You should include in your review relevant information from the film or book to allow your reader to follow your comments and evaluation.

(a) Begin your review with a brief summary of the content.
(b) Make reference to this content as necessary in your review.

UNIT FOUR

INTERACTION WITH THE READER
PRESENTING A POINT OF VIEW

Every written text expresses a point of view of some kind. This point of view can be communicated in a variety of ways. For example, the writer can choose to highlight certain facts which support his point of view while ignoring or downplaying others. The writer may also choose to present his facts subjectively or objectively. In a subjective presentation the writer's own feelings about the facts are readily revealed. In an objective presentaton, on the other hand, the writer suppresses his own feelings and relies on his choice of facts to convey his point of view. There is point of view of another kind – the writer's attitude to his reader – which is expressed in the tone of a piece of writing. This tone can, for instance, be polite, formal, distanced, familiar, rude or humorous. In practice, a mixture of such devices can be seen in any piece of writing.

TASK ONE

SELECTING AND INTERPRETING FACTS TO PRESENT A PARTICULAR POINT OF VIEW

This task shows how a writer may select and interpret facts to present a particular point of view. The same body of information can often successfully be used in such a way as to support a variety of viewpoints – even opposing ones.

These two tables show the results of a survey to compare the attitudes of older workers with those of younger workers conducted by a group of sociology students.

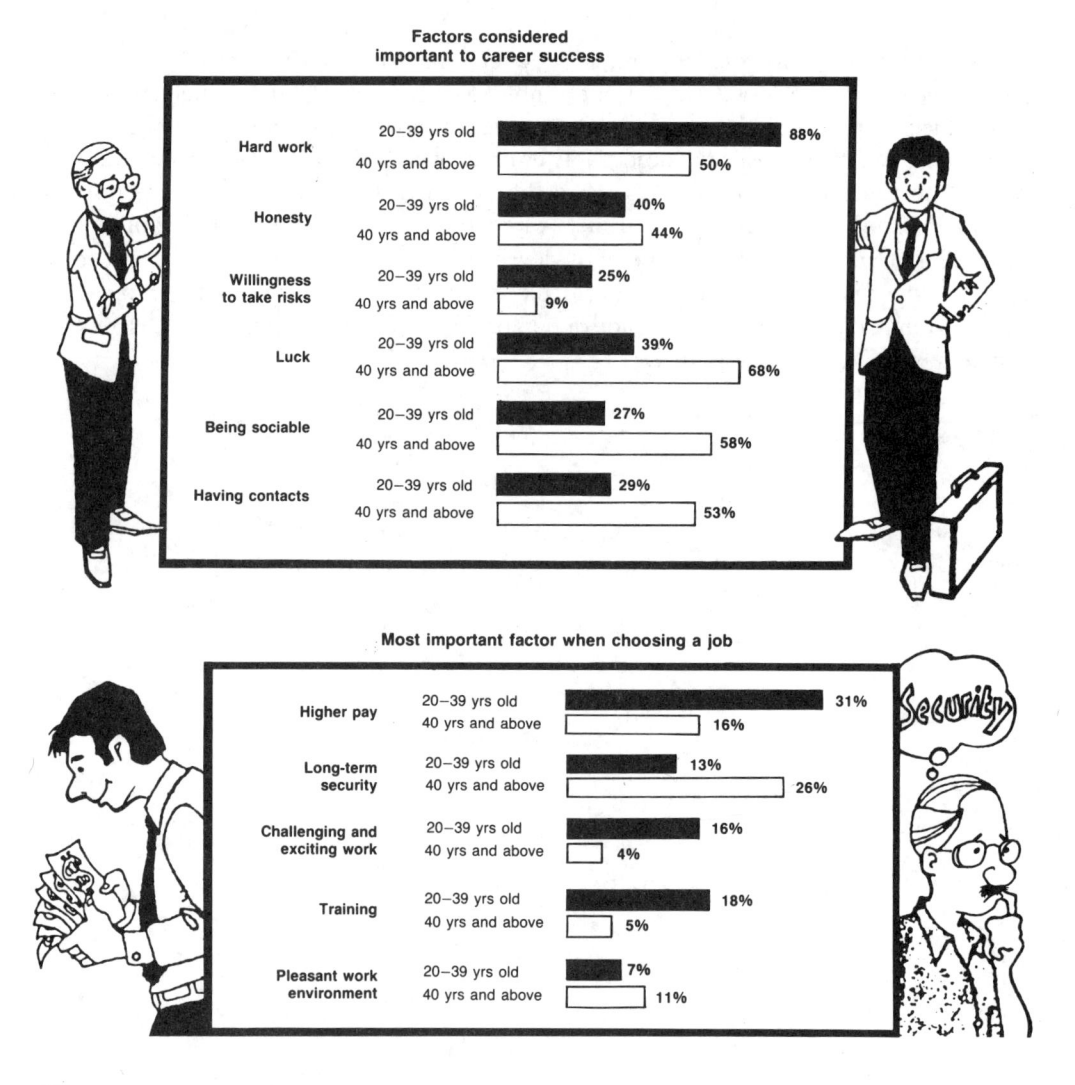

Factors considered important to career success

Factor	Age group	Percentage
Hard work	20–39 yrs old	88%
	40 yrs and above	50%
Honesty	20–39 yrs old	40%
	40 yrs and above	44%
Willingness to take risks	20–39 yrs old	25%
	40 yrs and above	9%
Luck	20–39 yrs old	39%
	40 yrs and above	68%
Being sociable	20–39 yrs old	27%
	40 yrs and above	58%
Having contacts	20–39 yrs old	29%
	40 yrs and above	53%

Most important factor when choosing a job

Factor	Age group	Percentage
Higher pay	20–39 yrs old	31%
	40 yrs and above	16%
Long-term security	20–39 yrs old	13%
	40 yrs and above	26%
Challenging and exciting work	20–39 yrs old	16%
	40 yrs and above	4%
Training	20–39 yrs old	18%
	40 yrs and above	5%
Pleasant work environment	20–39 yrs old	7%
	40 yrs and above	11%

Unit Four

1 Study the tables and then read the passage which follows where the writer uses the information to show that older workers make better employees.

A study of the results of this survey suggests that older workers are likely to make better employees than younger ones. This conclusion is based partly on a comparison of the views of these two groups of workers on factors contributing to career success. Honesty is more highly rated by older workers than by their younger counterparts, suggesting that older workers are likely to be more trustworthy. They are also more cautious in their approach to work, unlike younger workers, who are prone to take risks which can have disastrous consequences. In addition, the high value older workers place on being sociable points to their greater readiness to work for good relationships with other members of the workforce. There is no denying that a good working atmosphere is vital for the smooth operation of an organisation. This emphasis on sociability is also reflected in the importance older workers attach to having contacts. Both establishing and maintaining useful contacts are necessary in the modern business world.

Secondly, in terms of priorities in choosing a job, older workers show themselves to be more stable and committed than their younger counterparts. Not only are they less concerned about money, they are also much more realistic in their job expectations and consequently less likely to be frustrated on account of lack of excitement or challenge in their everyday work. All this, together with their interest in long-term security, means that older workers are more committed to the job they hold and less likely to move from one job to another in search of new stimulation. It is this commitment that older workers have to their job that perhaps argues most strongly in their favour as being better employees.

2 In small groups discuss these questions:
(a) Which items in the tables has the writer of this text left out? Why?
(b) Some of the items in the tables can easily be used to support the point of view that it is preferable to employ older workers. Which of the items used by the writer are like this?
(c) The other items that the writer has used could be interpreted in different ways so that they might favour either younger or older workers. Which items are of this type? How did the writer interpret them to support his point of view? How could each of these items be interpreted so as to favour younger workers?

3 As you have seen, the information in the two tables could be used to support very different points of view. Now, in your groups, discuss which items you would select and how you would interpret them to present one of the following viewpoints to your fellow students. One half of the class should discuss A and the other B.

    A: Neither older nor younger workers make better employees. (In other words, older and younger workers could simply be compared without favouring either group.)
    B: Younger workers are preferable as employees.

4 Individually, use the items you have selected to write a passage which presents the point of view you have discussed.

5 Join up with a student from the other half of the class and read each other's text.
(a) Has the writer made full use of the information in the tables to communicate his point of view?

(b) Has he left out any item which he could have used to his advantage?

With your partner, compare both your texts and discuss how they differ in terms of the selection and interpretation of information from the tables.

TASK TWO

PRESENTING INFORMATION: IMPERSONAL AND OBJECTIVE, PERSONALISED AND SUBJECTIVE

The two texts in this task illustrate two ways of presenting information. One of them is an example of an impersonal, objective presentation where the writer focuses on the facts and does not include personal comment. In other words, he allows the facts themselves to communicate his point of view. The other passage is a more personalised, subjective presentation which clearly shows the writer's feelings and contains overt evaluation of the information. The subject of both texts is the importation of foreign talent.

1 Read both the texts. Then in groups discuss the questions that follow.

Text One

Many developing countries employ foreign expertise in various areas of their infrastructure. Republic has not been unusual in this respect. However, in every aspect of the running of this country - not only in the Cabinet and Parliament but also in the upper echelons of the Civil Service, in the key posts in business and industry and in the top level appointments in the universities and schools - the percentage of Republic-born officials increased from 1960 to 1970 and has continued to increase up to the present. In 1960, 20% of the people in the higher ranks of government service were natives of Republic. This figure had increased to 57% in 1970 and to 72% by 1985.

Nevertheless, one may ask the question: Is there enough talent in Republic to maintain in the future the standards of leadership in the government and efficiency in the public service sector that have prevailed in the last 25 years? Is it wise to rely more and more on Republic-born people to fill all high level posts while at the same time reducing the numbers of foreign experts in these fields?

There is no doubt that the pool of talent in Republic is finite and limited. In the 1950's, when the average yearly birthrate was 60,000, approximately 60 extremely intelligent people were born each year. There was a similar I.Q. spread in the 1960's with approximately 50 highly intelligent people born out of a total of 50,000 per year. This is an average rate of 1 in 1,000. According to the Prime Minister, this average rate is even lower – 1 in 3,000 – when his criteria for good leadership – strong character, sound temperament and high motivation – are added. Furthermore, in the 1970's the annual birthrate fell to 40,000 and has continued to fall since then, further diminishing the number of intelligent people being born. The evaporation of the local talent pool will continue, because people with higher education have much smaller families than those with little or only primary education. The 1980 Census showed that women with tertiary education (who are likely to marry husbands with similar qualifications and to have children who will make it to university) had, on average, 1.6 children, while women with primary school qualifications had, on average, 2.7 and women with no educational qualification 3.6.

These facts and figures demonstrate the ever-diminishing size of Republic's talent pool and substantiate the argument for continuing to import foreign talent.

Text Two

We in Republic have, in common with many developing countries, employed a number of talented foreign nationals over the years. However, if we look at the people who have contributed to the running of this country, not only in government but also in the Civil Service, in business and industry and in education, over the past two and a half decades, we cannot fail to be pleasantly struck by the increasing number of locally born people occupying top positions. The percentage of Republic-born officials had increased from 20% in 1960 to a very satisfactory 72% by 1985. We can be proud that the rapid development of our country has been largely due to the able leadership provided by this increasing band of highly intelligent local people.

However, there must remain a certain degree of uneasiness in most peoples' minds as to whether there is enough talent in Republic to maintain the same high standards of leadership we have come to expect, especially as we continue to reduce the number of foreign experts in our country. The answer, sadly, is that there is not. The average yearly birthrate of 60,000 in the 1950's produced only about 60 extremely intelligent people. This same low average rate – about 1 in 1,000 – continues up to the present. Alas, not all of the people with good minds have the strong character, sound temperament and high motivation – qualities we look for in good leaders – to match their intellect. The number of people who do possess the necessary qualities works out to a mere 1 in 3,000. If we also take into consideration the fact that we are faced with a steadily falling birthrate today we can see that it is going to be impossible to maintain the pool of local talent.

The picture becomes even bleaker if we look at the spread of our population. Better educated people are producing much smaller families than those less well educated. The 1980 census showed that women with tertiary education had on average 1.6 children, while those with only primary education produced 2.7 and those with no education 3.6. Unfortunately, there is no denying that it is the well educated families who are likely to produce the exceptionally bright children needed.

It seems that it is no longer possible for us to continue to rely more and more on local talent for the brain power to lead Republic. With such a rapidly diminishing pool of local talent it is essential for us to accept the desirability of encouraging more, not fewer, able, talented people to come to work in our country. We have to make these people feel welcome and wanted so that they will make this their permanent home and contribute to our future progress.

(a) Both of these writers share the same point of view about bringing foreign talent into Republic. What is it?
(b) In Text Two the writer says 'we *cannot fail* to be *pleasantly* struck by the increasing number of locally born people occupying top positions.' Here he is clearly showing us what he feels about the facts. Underline the parts of either text which express the writer's personal feelings about the situation or evaluation of the facts.
(c) Bearing in mind the parts of the texts you underlined in your discussion of (b), what do you think is the main difference in the way the information is presented in the two texts?

TASK THREE

FURTHER OBJECTIVE AND SUBJECTIVE PRACTICE

This very subjective piece of writing comes from a holiday brochure for Pulau Tioman, Malaysia. As you read it, notice how the writer has expressed his feelings about the information he presents. By doing this he fulfils his purpose for writing, which is to make this island appear as attractive a holiday destination as possible.

The biggest attraction of this lovely island (which featured as Bali H'ai in the movie *South Pacific*) is its wonderful beaches fringing beautiful clear blue waters. Swimming, windsurfing, fishing and sailing are all great here. Snorkelling and skin-diving are popular as well. The abundance of magnificent, colourful sea-life makes the island a prime destination for both amateur and experienced divers, who can hire first-class equipment on the island.

Tioman is actually the biggest of 64 islands offshore from Mersing, so it has much more to offer than sea sports alone. There are ten villages on the island, eight of which can be reached on foot. The visitor will find a warm reception at any of these.

Nature lovers will find Tioman a paradise. Plenty of local flora and fauna can be spotted while exploring jungle paths and there are several treks that the experienced hiker will not disdain.

Pulau Tioman's sole resort hotel, the Tioman Island Resort, sprawls across beautifully landscaped gardens. It has 74 deluxe, superior and standard rooms plus 45 chalets. All the rooms are tastefully furnished and many have breathtaking sea views. The most attractive feature of the hotel is the brand new swimming pool with its cleverly designed bar area reminiscent of a lovely old Malay *kampong** house. Other water sports like waterskiing, boating or cruising around the island in Malaysia's first-ever glass-bottom boat, from which you can look at a myriad of fantastic rainbow fish, are also available at this resort.

For those who wish to relax, the pearly white beaches lined with shady palm trees make a perfect place to laze, take long strolls or picnic with your family.

Although this exquisite island is most easily accessible from Mersing, it can also be reached by boat from Kuantan or by a pleasant, short flight from Kuala Lumpur or Singapore (see map).

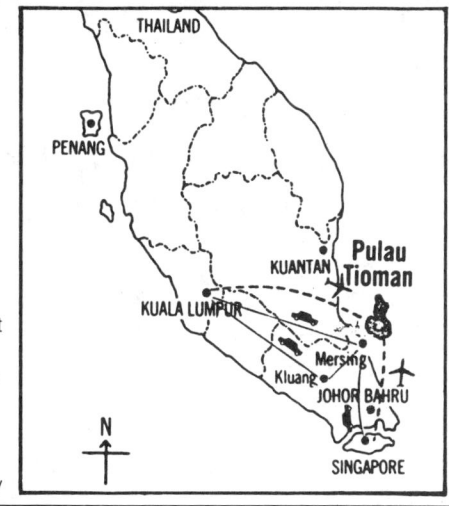

**kampong* – village

1 With a partner underline all the facts in the passage, i.e. all the bits of the text that do not contain any expression of the writer's feelings, e.g. 'The biggest attraction of this lovely island (which featured as Bali H'ai in the movie *South Pacific*) is its wonderful beaches fringing beautiful clear blue waters'.

2 Together, use the facts to write a more objective paragraph for a travel guide. Your reader needs information but not your opinions.

3 Now, still working together, think of something you are familiar with, e.g. another holiday resort, a useful gadget, a house or other property. First, make a list of all the facts about the item and then think of ways in which the facts could be presented to make the item appear as attractive as possible. Write two descriptions of the item. The first should be a straight-forward description for somebody who is unfamiliar with it, and the second a more subjective presentation for an advertising brochure or catalogue.

TASK FOUR

RELATIONSHIP AND ATTITUDE TO THE READER

In this task you will look at the use of tone in a text. Tone reflects your view of your relationship to your reader as well as your attitude to him. The relationship may, for example, be distant, formal, close or familiar and the attitude could be polite, respectful, deferential, rude or authoritative. Your attitude could also reflect the degree of personal interest or concern you have for your reader. The tone you use determines to a large extent how your reader will respond to your writing and therefore you should remember to consider tone in every text you write. Here you will study tone in a letter of complaint and in some possible replies to it.

1 First read these two versions of a letter and then, in groups, answer the questions which follow.

Letter One

```
                                        76 Peace Road
                                        Republic 1129

                                        25 February 1987

Director
Building Control Division
Public Works Department
Government Road
Republic 0106

Dear Sir

I am writing to you concerning the building operations which
are in progress on a site adjoining my property. Since the
work first started, the situation has become worse and worse.
It is now unreasonable to expect anyone to continue to put up
with it.

Firstly, the noise level is now intolerably high throughout
the day. This is particularly annoying as work starts at 6:30
am and often does not finish until after 7:00 pm. Worse still,
the work is carried out not only on weekdays but also on
Sundays and public holidays. This is a residential area.
Surely the residents are entitled to some peace and quiet at
such times?

Secondly, a temporary building to house the workmen has just
been erected immediately on the other side of my boundary
hedge. This I find totally unacceptable since the building is
situated only nineteen feet from my bedroom, bathroom and
study windows thus reducing the light and blocking the view
from these three rooms entirely. In addition, being so close,
the noise from the site will not be restricted to building
operations alone or to the day time work period. There must be
a law in this country which prohibits the construction of a
building at such close proximity. I am surprised that the
Public Works Department, which should be responsible for
building control, does not seem to be aware of such a law.

I expect the appropriate section of your department to look
into this immediately and ensure that the workers' quarters
are relocated, that work does not begin earlier than 8:00 am
and that it is prohibited on Sundays and public holidays.

I look forward to receiving an early reply.

Yours faithfully
A. Neighbour (Ms)
```

Task Four

Letter Two

76 Peace Road
Republic 1129

25 February 1987

Director
Building Control Division
Public Works Department
Government Road
Republic 0106

Dear Sir

I have been advised to write to you concerning the building operations which are in progress on a site adjoining my property. Recently the situation has become most annoying for the following reasons.

Firstly, the noise level is now extremely high throughout the day, which is disturbing as work starts at 6:30 am and often does not finish until after 7:00 pm. In addition, work continues on Sundays and public holidays, which, I believe, may not be legal in the middle of a residential area.

Secondly, a temporary building to house the workmen has just been erected immediately on the other side of my boundary hedge. This I find particularly unpleasant since the building is situated only nineteen feet from my bedroom, bathroom and study windows so that it reduces the light and blocks the view from these three windows entirely. In addition, being so close, noise from the site will not be restricted to building operations alone or to the daytime work period.

I should be extremely grateful if the appropriate section of your department could look into this matter and consider relocating the workers' quarters, restricting work to after 8:00 am and prohibiting it on Sundays and public holidays.

Yours faithfully
A. Neighbour (Ms)

(a) Do the writer and recipient know each other?
(b) Have they had any previous correspondence?
(c) What information does the writer give about the situation? The facts are the same in both letters – note down these facts.
(d) In the first letter the writer says 'the situation has become *worse and worse.*' This clearly expresses her own feelings. Underline other parts in both letters where the writer expresses her own attitude to the facts. What is the difference between the two letters with regard to the way the writer's feelings are expressed?
(e) What does the writer hope to achieve? Where does she state this? What is the difference in her request as stated in Letter One and Letter Two?
(f) On a scale of 1–5 how would you describe the tone of each letter in each of the following areas?

Polite	5	4	3	2	1	Impolite
Demanding	5	4	3	2	1	Requesting
Formal	5	4	3	2	1	Informal

(g) Given what you have deduced about the situation, the communication and the people involved, which letter do you think is the most appropriate? Give reasons.

2   Now read these three possible replies.

Reply One

> **Public Works Department**
>
> Dear Madam
>
> I acknowledge receipt of your letter of 25 February 1987. Your complaints have been investigated.
>
> The architect will restrict the working hours to between 7:00 am and 7:00 pm in accordance with his permit. For your information, building operations on Sundays and public holidays are legal. The work on this site will only last thirteen months.
>
> The workmen's quarters will be demolished.
>
> Yours faithfully
> *Cynthia Lingam*
> Cynthia Lingam

Task Four

Reply Two

Public Works Department

Dear Ms Neighbour

Many thanks for your letter of 25 February. I am terribly sorry to hear that you are having such problems and I hope we can do something to help you.

I have had a word with the architect in charge of the site and reminded him that the time of building work must be kept between 7:00 am and 7:00 pm as we told him when we issued the permit to start work. I am sorry, but according to the law we cannot tell the contractor not to work on Sundays and public holidays. The work is only going to last thirteen months anyway.

As for the workmen's quarters, I quite agree with you that this is unacceptable and you will be very happy to know that it will be pulled down more or less immediately. I hope all this meets with your approval and that things will improve.

Yours very truly

Bartholomew B. Snaddon

Reply Three

> **Public Works Department**
>
> Dear Ms Neighbour
>
> Thank you for your letter of 25 February. The problems you mention have been investigated and the following measures taken.
>
> The architect in charge of the site has been informed that the time of building work must be kept between 7:00 am and 7:00 pm as was stated when the permit to commence work was issued. I am sorry to inform you that the continuation of building operations on Sundays and public holidays is within the law. However, the duration of the work is only expected to be thirteen months.
>
> With regard to the workmen's quarters, I am pleased to inform you that the unauthorized building is to be demolished immediately.
>
> Please do not hesitate to contact this office should you have any further queries.
>
> Yours sincerely
>
> Janet Snow

3 In your groups describe the tone of each letter of reply in terms of:
(a) Politeness – which letters are the most/least polite?
(b) Formality – which letters are the most/least formal?
(c) Concern (degree of understanding or sympathy) – which letters express the most/least concern for Ms Neighbour?

Find specific evidence for your description.

Considering the relationship between the writer and the reader and the nature of the communication, which reply do you think is most appropriate? Why?

TASK FIVE

ASSESSMENT OF TOPIC, PURPOSE IN WRITING AND
RELATIONSHIP WITH THE READER

To produce a letter of appropriate tone you must take into consideration what feelings you wish to communicate to your reader. This requires a careful assessment of your topic, purpose in writing, and the relationship you want to create or maintain with the reader.

1   Read this letter of complaint and the memo which follows it.

```
                                          3 Bridge Street
                                          Gunnerville, 3583
                                          Victoria
                                          Australia

                                          15 December 1987

The Manager
Viva East Travel Agency
62 Westway Road
Republic 2142

Dear Sir

     My wife and I have just returned from a tour of the East,
organized in part by your travel agency.  Though we enjoyed
much of our overseas trip we found the Republic section to be
very disappointing for the following reasons.
     The type of accommodation was nowhere of the high quality
outlined in the brochure - a copy of which I have enclosed
with the relevant sections underlined.
     Although the trips to the rural areas were quite
interesting, the standard of accommodation was even worse than
it was in the city - in some cases quite deplorable.
     Furthermore, there was no one to guide us as to where to
eat - the driver/guide seemed to disappear as soon as we
arrived at our destination.
     Finally, it seems to me that a trip to the east coast of
Republic is extremely unwise in the monsoon season - a fact
that was not made known to us beforehand.
     On the whole this section of the tour was not well
thought out or organised and is one that I would not
recommend.

Yours faithfully

Simon Whelan
```

This letter was forwarded to the tour organiser who sent the manager the following memo in response to the complaint.

Intrepid Explorers

MEMO

TO: Manager
FROM: Tour Organizer
SUBJECT: Complaint letter of 15 December 1987
DATE: 29 December 1987

- this is the only complaint we have received.
- the hotels were the same as always.
- this fellow was a complainer – a nuisance to everyone on the trip.
- the monsoon came early – not our fault – tours are not held in the predicted monsoon season.
- the driver is new – from all other reports he is very good.
- the tour is the Budget Tour – what does he expect for such a low cost?

---

2 Your task is to use this memo to write an appropriate reply to the complaint. You will obviously have to convert the bluntness of the memo to a tone more suitable for company-to-client correspondence. In particular, make sure that your letter:

- Does not offend the customer.
- Expresses regret about his dissatisfaction.
- Reassures the reader about the efficiency and reputation of the agency and the people who work for it.

3 Exchange letters with another student and see if the guidelines above have been followed.

4 Revise your own letter in the light of your partner's comments.

TASK SIX

PRESENTING A POINT OF VIEW

Use what you have learned in this unit about presenting a point of view to write a text about a problem which you see existing or emerging in your country.

1 In small groups discuss some problems you see existing or emerging in your country today (e.g. a rapidly increasing number of elderly people, drug taking, brain drain, etc.). Select one of these for further discussion. You should clearly identify and describe the problem as you see it today, its causes and the way it is likely to affect your country in the future if no attempt is made to deal with it adequately. Make note of all the facts that come out of your discussion.

2 Individually, choose what kind of text you want to write (e.g. an academic paper, a letter to a newspaper or to a friend studying abroad, an article for a magazine, etc.). Decide what your purpose in writing is and be clear about who your expected reader(s) will be. Then:

- Decide what your point of view is with regard to the problem.
- In your discussion a lot of points will have been raised. Choose the facts which are most useful to present your point of view.
- Decide whether you feel a subjective or objective presentation of the facts best suits your purpose for writing.
- Make sure the tone is one suitable for the feelings you wish to communicate to your reader.

UNIT FIVE

INTERACTION WITH THE READER
ANTICIPATING THE READER'S RESPONSE

When putting forward a written argument to support a point of view it is important to remember that the reader may not share the same point of view and may object to the argument presented. To present an effective and convincing argument the writer must not make exaggerated claims and must anticipate and deal with possible objections or counter-arguments. This shows that he has considered all aspects of the case.

Preliminary Preparation for Task Five

For Task Five you are asked to find a short statement or opinion with which you disagree. This can be on any subject and may come from any source, for example, something you have heard on the radio or television, or a statement made by a relative, teacher or friend. Some examples include:

1. 'Boys don't need to help with the housework.' (Spoken by a student's brother.)
2. 'God is not as lively as, say, a few thousand years ago.' (A university professor quoted in a newspaper.)

Be prepared to explain why you disagree with the statement you choose.

TASK ONE

ARGUMENT AND COUNTER-ARGUMENT

The text you read here, about student evaluation of lecturers, is from a student newspaper. It is an example of a successful presentation of argument and counter-argument. You can see how the writer has carefully considered the possible objections his reader might raise to his arguments and attempted to deal with them.

OPINION

Would you describe the lecturer's presentation as:

| Very interesting | Quite interesting | Satisfactory | Boring | ?

Do his lectures teach you:

| A lot | Quite a lot | Something | Nothing | ?

Anyone who has ever attended a university knows that the quality of lecturers varies greatly. A few are very effective communicators, conveying the substance of their lectures clearly and interestingly and inspiring students to want to know more about the subject. Others produce dull, rambling and sometimes even incoherent lectures from which the students learn little and which are likely to kill any interest they may have in the subject. Lecturing is a major part of a university lecturer's job and it would seem reasonable that effectiveness in this task should be a major criterion in assessing a lecturer for promotion, tenure and so on. However, it is very often the case that far more weight is given to such factors as participation in research, number of publications and even performance of administrative duties. It is my contention that a lecturer's performance in the lecture hall should be regularly evaluated and that the best people to carry out this evaluation are those directly on the receiving end – the students.

It could, of course, be argued that students, particularly undergraduates, are not competent to evaluate the academic quality of lectures. They may know little of the subject and have no means of judging whether a particular lecturer is giving them outdated or irrelevant information and concepts or whether he or she is accurately reflecting the current state of the discipline. If anyone should evaluate lecturers, the argument goes, it should be their colleagues. However, I am not arguing that students should be asked to comment upon the academic content of lectures. The academic calibre of lecturers can still be assessed in the usual way through their qualifications, publications, course outlines, performance at staff seminars and so on. What students are best placed to do is to evaluate the effectiveness of the teaching which goes on in a lecture. Lecturers often have little time to regularly attend one another's lectures. Moreover, their comments are likely to be affected by personal or academic prejudices. Students, on the other hand, know perfectly well when they are learning something and are normally quite clear about which lectures are interesting and give them a clear understanding of the subject and which are boring and leave them baffled.

Another common objection is that the students do not know what is good for them. They are likely to rate highly lecturers who do not demand much of them, who keep their lectures very simple, give few assignments and award good grades for mediocre work. They might even be influenced by such irrelevant factors as whether a lecturer is good looking or how friendly he or she is. This argument assumes very low levels of maturity, motivation and intelligence among students.

University students, after all, are no longer school children. They come to the university to learn and normally expect a certain amount of stimulation and challenge. Anyone who has mixed with undergraduates will know how critical they can be of lectures which are uninspiring, dull or too elementary. I am certain that most students care far too much about the quality of education they receive at university to treat the evaluation of lecturers as a mere popularity contest.

I suspect that many of the objections to student evaluation of lecturers stem from the fear some lecturers have of being subject to criticism by their students. However, lecturers should see such evaluation as an opportunity to become aware of defects in their lecturing techniques and thus to become better lecturers. Such a system could benefit both students and lecturers as well as help department heads to more realistically assess the strengths and weaknesses of their teaching staff.

1 Look at paragraph one. Here the author introduces his main argument.

(a) What is it?
(b) Where is it placed in the paragraph?
(c) Why do you think it has been placed there?

2 Look at paragraphs two and three. Here the writer anticipates the reader's possible objections or counter-arguments to his views.

(a) What are these objections?
(b) What wording does the writer use to show that he is not presenting his own point of view?
(c) Find the place where each objection ends and the writer starts to deal with it. He does this in one of two ways:
  (i) by showing that an objection does not apply to the argument he is putting forward, or
  (ii) by criticising a counter-argument and pointing out its shortcomings.
  Which objection is dealt with in the way described in (i)? Which is dealt with in the way described in (ii)?

3 Look at paragraph four. A good conclusion to a text putting forward an argument often does more than simply restate the writer's main contentions. Here the writer looks again at both the counter-arguments he has discussed to see what they have in common.

(a) Why does he feel people raise these objections?
(b) Does his conclusion present any additional argument in his favour? If so, what?
(c) How does this strengthen his case?

4 Discussion questions:

(a) Are the author's arguments in favour of students' evaluations convincing? Can you think of any other arguments he might use?
(b) Can you think of any other objections or counter-arguments?

TASK TWO

PRESENTING A CONVINCING ARGUMENT ANTICIPATING THE READER'S RESPONSE

These two texts are first drafts of students' essays on the subject of caring for old people. They both fail to present a convincing argument because they do not anticipate the reader's response in some way.

1   Read both essays.

Essay One

```
                                         Alphonso Hidalgo
                                    English Composition 100
                                                   Group 4

With modern advances in medical science, our average life span
has been substantially increased.  This increase, however, has
brought in its wake a serious family and social problem,  the
problem of an increasing number of old people who are unable
to run their own homes or take care of themselves and who are
forced to rely on everybody around them,  especially their
family.  The right thing to do is , of course, to put them in
homes for the aged.  Unfortunately old people are not prepared
to accept the fact that they are not as capable as they used
to be and need to be under the care that such homes offer.
```

62   Unit Five

Most old people prefer to live with their grown-up son or daughter. However, there are many problems with living with old people. One major problem is the difference in attitude and way of life between people of two different generations. In this fast changing world, our attitudes and ways of life are very different from those of the past. Old people, however, are not prepared to accept or adapt themselves to these changes. Instead, they cling to their old beliefs, attitudes and ways of life, firmly believing that if people of the younger generation cannot agree with them it is the result of their inexperience. With this attitude, old people generally expect those younger than they are to defer to them in all matters. This naturally creates considerable strain and is the cause of much discord.

Apart from being a source of strain and conflict in the home, old people are difficult to live with because of their dependence on others. Old people can often be physically inactive and lethargic and even when they are capable of doing things for themselves, they are unwilling to exert themselves and prefer to be waited on. As for those who are infirm, they are, needless to say, a considerable burden on those they live with.

Above all, old people are difficult to live with because they believe they have a special claim on their grown-up sons and daughters, arguing that they have given them their very life and have worked hard to bring them up. What these old people have not realised is that giving birth to their children was in most cases not the result of deliberate choice, especially in the past when contraceptive devices were unknown. It was by accident, as it were, that their children were born into this world. And having thus brought them into this world, it was their responsibility to bring them up, a responsibility they should not and could not shirk. They were doing no more than what they owed their children and should therefore not expect any return. After all, bringing up children is a joy, a fulfilment, a reward in itself.

Having thus examined the problems of living with aged parents, and the "debt" children owe to their parents, it seems clear that parents are being selfish in refusing to go to homes for the aged. In such institutions, old people can enjoy the company of others of their own age and so conflicts resulting from differences of attitude or way of life do not arise. Furthermore, such homes also provide excellent nursing care, as people with special training are employed for this purpose. Indeed those who argue that it is heartless for grown-up sons and daughters to place their aged parents in such institutions are just being unrealistic and sentimental.

Essay Two

>   Evan Kwee
>   Eng. Comp. 100
>   Group 4
>
> The problem of what to do with elderly parents is one that is faced by most people. What is generally obvious is that most families do not live successfully with elderly grandparents. Elderly people have specific needs and wants which cannot always be met in a hectic modern home. They also have different philosophies and lifestyles that clash with those around them. Although parents do not wish to neglect or mistreat their own parents, they realise that their first duty is to their own children and when tension and conflict arise it is the grandparents who will be blamed and the children who will suffer. So, what are the solutions to this problem?
>
> A possible one is to separate the generations — admit to the fact that the three generation household does not work. Many have argued that parents and children benefit from close and constant contact with people outside the "nuclear unit" — grandparents, aunts and uncles, cousins and neighbours, and that living in an atmosphere of three generations is something that can only benefit everyone. The tensions of child rearing that so often plague parents are dissipated by the presence of grandparents — not only as ready-made babysitters who can ensure a quick escape for a child-free evening out — but also as people whose needs and idiosyncracies have to be considered. Children learn how to cope with people of a different age and outlook, in short, they learn tolerance for and acceptance of others.
>
> A danger in discussing the problem of old people is to readily assume that they want to live with their children. It is often maintained that they are, at best, an educational tool for teenagers or, at worst, a problem that just has to be accepted until it is solved (i.e. until they die). They apparently do not have their own wants, wishes, dreams, desires, frustrations, etc. and they are only too willing to give up their rights to a free life to fit in with others.
>
> A more practical solution to the situation is to set up retirement villages — places which enable

> people to live in separate houses or flats but where there are community eating facilities and 24 hours medical care. Residents can engage village cleaners and maintenance staff if they wish, or they are free to do their own household chores. They are free to come and go as they please yet they can transfer themselves to a village nursing home if they feel that they cannot look after themselves.

2 Working in small groups, look at the essays more closely to answer these questions about each of them.

(a) What is the main suggestion put forward by the writer as the central theme of the essay?
(b) Does the writer take into account any possible objections to his viewpoint? Give examples.
(c) If the writer has considered any objections, are they adequately dealt with? Give examples.
(d) Are there some points made in the argument that are exaggerated to the extent of being unconvincing? Give examples.

Discuss your answers with the rest of the class. Which text presents a more effective argument? Why? In what ways could the student improve this essay in his final draft?

TASK THREE

DEALING WITH COUNTER-ARGUMENTS

This task is based on two possible introductions to a text which presents a particular argument. You will have a chance to practise dealing with counter-arguments by writing the rest of the text.

The following two introductions show two arguments regarding the dropping of an atomic bomb on Hiroshima* in 1945.

Introduction to Text One
The Japanese and the Americans are still arguing over the bombing of Hiroshima. To the Americans, Hiroshima represents an unfortunate but ultimately humane military action.

---

* On 6 August 1945 Hiroshima, a seaport in southwest Japan, was hit by the world's first atomic bomb, dropped by the United States Air Force. On 10 August 1945 the city of Nagasaki was the target of a second bomb. Immediately after this the Japanese emperor surrendered and World War II ended.

Introduction to Text Two
The Japanese and the Americans are still arguing over the bombing of Hiroshima. To the Japanese, Hiroshima represents a calculated and inhumane experiment in destruction.

1 Working in small groups, discuss the points that follow. Identify those points which can be used in favour of and those which can be used against each of the arguments introduced above.

(a) Attack made to save two million Allied lives by shortening World War II.
(b) Over 80,000 people killed.
(c) Japanese belief: bomb dropped on Hiroshima to test effects under ideal conditions (densely populated city hemmed in by mountains and sea).
(d) Long-term effects of radiation at Hiroshima: not significant number of radiation-related abnormalities (based on study of 70,000 children conceived after the bomb and born of exposed parents).
(e) Hiroshima bombed flat: many people died or suffered severe injuries.

Are there other points relevant to the topic? What are they?

2 Choose one of the introductions given at the beginning of this task. Using points you discussed in (1), individually write a short text in which you present your argument and effectively deal with possible counter-arguments to it. Be sure to include an appropriate conclusion. Your text is to appear in a student magazine doing a feature issue on the debate surrounding the use of nuclear weapons.

3 Exchange your text with another student and evaluate how effectively the argument has been presented and whether counter-arguments have been effectively dealt with.

TASK FOUR

ELABORATING A PERSONAL VIEWPOINT: ANTICIPATING AND DEALING WITH COUNTER-ARGUMENTS

In this task you will be practising the expression of an argument that elaborates a personal viewpoint as well as anticipating and dealing with counter-arguments.

1 Read this article. It has been adapted from *Newsweek* magazine.

SCIENCE

A Choice in the Womb

A pregnant woman who learns that she risks having a defective child can choose to have an abortion. But what if she finds that she is carrying twins, one of which seems normal, while the other has a serious defect? A team of New York doctors reported just such a case recently and described how they killed the abnormal foetus* in the womb† and later presided over the successful birth of the healthy brother.

The forty-year-old patient had been overjoyed on learning that she was pregnant for the first time. But because of her age she ran an increased risk of having a defective child so she was given detailed tests which showed that one of the foetuses had the extra chromosome that is the hallmark of mongolism.‡ She and her husband faced an agonising choice: whether to have a conventional abortion and destroy both the normal and the abnormal foetuses, or continue the pregnancy and raise a retarded child. They decided on an abortion – unless they could find specialists who would try a difficult and almost unprecedented technique to save the normal foetus and, in effect, abort the abnormal one.

Doctors Thomas Kerenyi and Usha Chitkara of the Mount Sinai School of Medicine were willing to try. But first they carefully explained the risks. The operation could lead to an abortion of both foetuses, or a difficult premature delivery for the healthy one and other possible complications. Worst of all, since there were no definite 'markers' to distinguish one twin from the other, the physicians might possibly kill the wrong foetus. The procedure had been carried out successfully only once before. Nonetheless, the parents decided to take the chance.

The physicians used the most sophisticated modern medical devices to guide them in the operation. They found that the position of the two twins had not changed much since the initial test, increasing the chance that they had found the right target. The abnormal foetus was lying across the mother's pelvis with its head on the left side.

Having administered a local anaesthetic the physicians inserted a long needle into the mother's abdomen and removed the fluid from the affected twin's sac before pressing the needle into the foetus's chest. However, they missed its heart, which – at twenty weeks of gestation – was only about the size of an apple seed. With the second attempt the needle punctured the heart and 25 millilitres of blood, about half the total blood volume, were removed. Suddenly the heart stopped beating and the foetus became still. The twin was not affected.

Three days later tests confirmed that the physicians had killed the foetus with mongolism. Follow-up scans showed that the normal one was growing while the dead foetus was shrivelling. After twenty weeks the mother gave birth to a healthy boy, who is still doing well. The brother was delivered as a paper-thin remnant of tissues. It is not uncommon for a woman to carry a dead foetus to term§ – and the risks to the mother's health are not great.

Describing the case in the *New England Journal of Medicine*, Kerenyi and Chitkara emphasised that they had left the decision to undergo a 'selective birth' entirely up to the parents. The family, says Dr Kurt Hirshhorn, who is chairman of Mt Sinai's paediatrics department, 'must decide what choices are right for them.' But 'out of an abundance of caution,' the doctors added, the hospital obtained a court ruling confirming the mother's right to decide to destroy one foetus while preserving the life of the other twin.

Adapted from 'A Choice in the Womb', *Newsweek*, 29 June 1981, Matt Clark with Linda R. Prout; copyright 1981 Newsweek Inc. All rights reserved. Reprinted by permission.

*foetus: an unborn child developing inside the mother.

†womb: the part of the mother's body where an unborn child is carried.

‡mongolism: an abnormality which results in mental retardation and various physical deformities.

§to carry to term: to deliver a child after a normal period of pregnancy.

2 Decide what your reaction to the article is. Do you think such an operation is justified or not? Divide yourselves into groups according to your viewpoint.

3 In your groups note down some points that support your viewpoint. Also write down some points that you feel could be used *against* your argument. You may like to use some of the discussion points below. In the writing task that is to follow you have to deal with both your viewpoint and the viewpoint of those who would disagree with you.

Discussion points
The following points relate to abortion, mongolism and the operation described in the *Newsweek* article. You may find some of them useful in anticipating possible counter-arguments.

(a) Mongolism is more than retardation. It is marked by structural deformities in the heart, intestines and lungs. It also usually means a shortened life span.
(b) Every family has the right to decide what choices are the best for them.
(c) Abortion is murder.
(d) The birth of a mongoloid twin may lead to traumatic experiences for the normal child.
(e) The operation of 'selective abortion' included an irresponsible risk to the life of the normal twin.
(f) The birth of such twins would mean an enormous emotional, financial and physical burden on any parents.
(g) Are surgeons just experimenting with lives?
(h) Mongoloid children are often happy and affectionate.
(i) The fifth of the Ten Commandments states: 'Thou shalt not kill'.
(j) Are parents in the sort of situation outlined in the article too emotionally involved to make a rational decision?

4 In your groups plan a letter to be written to the editor of *Newsweek* expressing your views on the issues raised in the article 'A Choice in the Womb'. You have to recognise that counter-arguments exist and that you need to deal with them when writing this letter.

5 Individually write a letter to *Newsweek*.

6 Exchange letters with another student, preferably someone whose viewpoint is different from yours. Evaluate the presentation of both arguments and counter-arguments. Read an example of argument and counter-argument from one of your letters to the rest of the class.

TASK FIVE

DISAGREEING

For this task, you will need the statement you were asked to collect at the beginning of this unit. You have to explain why you disagree with it. In doing so, you will need to deal effectively with the major arguments that could be used to support the statement.

1 Form small groups. Each student in turn should present his or her statement to the group explaining clearly why he or she disagrees with it. The other students in the group should point out any weaknesses in the presenter's argument and bring up as many counter-arguments as they can.

2 Now individually write a text, to be read by one of the students from another group, presenting your argument against the statement you collected. Take into account and deal with the major counter-arguments raised by your group so that your reader can see the reasonableness of your position.

3 Exchange your text with a student from another group. In evaluating one another's texts you should consider:

(a) Whether the points made in the argument are exaggerated.
(b) Whether all the major counter-arguments have been taken into account.
(c) Whether each counter-argument has been effectively dealt with.
(d) Whether the writer's own opinion is clearly expressed and well supported.

TASK SIX

ARGUING FOR OR AGAINST

'With modern technology we are moving skywards.'

Using this statement as your central theme, write an address which could be given at the opening of a 'Museum of the Twentieth Century'. You may choose to agree or disagree with the statement. In either case you will need to take into account opposing viewpoints. You might like to use some of Professor Brainstorm's ideas.

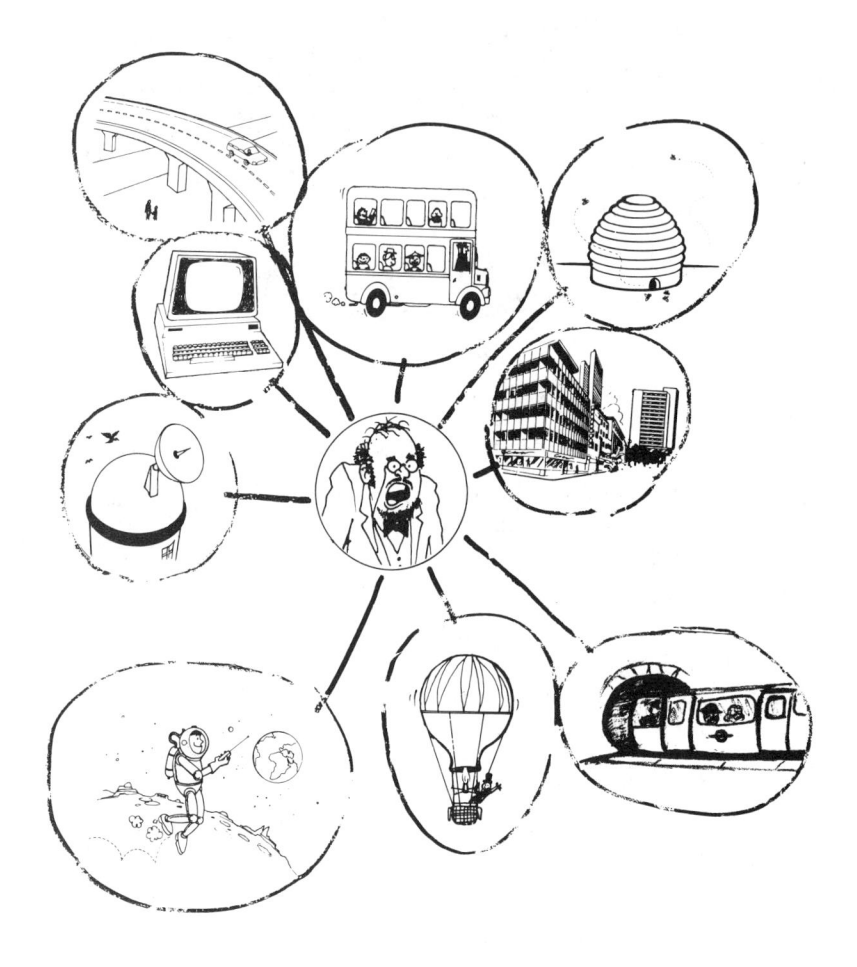

APPENDIX ONE

LAKE NIOS – TEXT WITH REVISION NOTATION

①One theory of how the disaster happened is that it was the result of volcanic activity. ~~This activity originated~~ *originating* from a volcano situated next to Lake Nios, which was the site of the eruption. [At the foot of the volcano by the shore of the lake is the town of Wum,] *irrelevant* (and on the opposite shore are a *combine with sentence ②* number of other settlements.) ②At the time of year when the eruption took place, the wind was blowing, in the direction of the settlements (from the lake). *word order* *on the shore opposite the volcano.* ③What must have happened was that *the* volcanic activity caused a *activity already mentioned* *Article —* sudden release of gases produced from hot molten matter underground. ④These gases, which most probably included hydrogen sulphide, carbon dioxide and carbon monoxide, were blown in clouds over the lake towards the settlements. [The bottom of the lake is made up of layers of hardened lava between which pockets of gas were trapped and collected over many years.] *omit*

Appendix One 71

APPENDIX TWO

ALLIGATOR RIVER

Once there was a poor woman named Abigail who was in love with a poor man named Gregory. They had been engaged for two years and were planning to get married as soon as they had saved enough gold to pay for the ceremony and wedding party. Gregory lived on the shore of a river. Abigail lived on the opposite shore of the river. Every day, Abigail would visit Gregory on his side of the river, which was easy to do since there was a bridge spanning the river.

Everything was fine until a storm caused the bridge to be washed away. Naturally, Abigail missed seeing Gregory, and missed him even more since the bridge was not replaced. The destroyed bridge alone wouldn't have been a big problem because the river was not very deep or wide and could be crossed easily by a good swimmer. Abigail was a good swimmer. However, she could not swim as fast as the alligators which lived in the river. She would certainly have been eaten if she had attempted to swim across the river.

Days went by. Weeks went by without Abigail being able to see Gregory. Then one day she saw a boatman with a boat on the river. The boatman's name was Sinbad. Abigail explained her problem to Sinbad and asked if he would take her across the river. Sinbad knew about the gold that she and Gregory had been saving. He said that he would take her across if she gave him all the gold they had saved. She promptly refused and went to a friend named Ivan to see if he could help her with the boatman. Ivan listened to the whole story and then said he didn't want to get involved in the situation at all. Abigail felt her only alternative was to accept Sinbad's terms. So, she gave him all their gold and he took Abigail across the river and she was able to see Gregory.

Abigail, who never kept anything from Gregory, told him about giving Sinbad their gold in order to cross the river. Gregory was furious when he heard the story and threw her out of his house. Heartsick and dejected, Abigail told Simon, an old friend of hers, everything that had happened. Simon was shocked by the behaviour of Gregory and felt sorry for Abigail. He sought Gregory out and beat him brutally. Abigail was sad at seeing Gregory being beaten up. As our story ends, we hear Abigail crying over her misfortune.

ENGLISH LANGUAGE UNIT
APPLIED LANGUAGES CENTRE
UNIVERSITY OF BATH,
CLAVERTON DOWN,
BATH, BA2 7AY,
GREAT BRITAIN.